MW00559568

Country Inn

BARB ADAMS AND ALMA ALLEN
OF BLACKBIRD DESIGNS

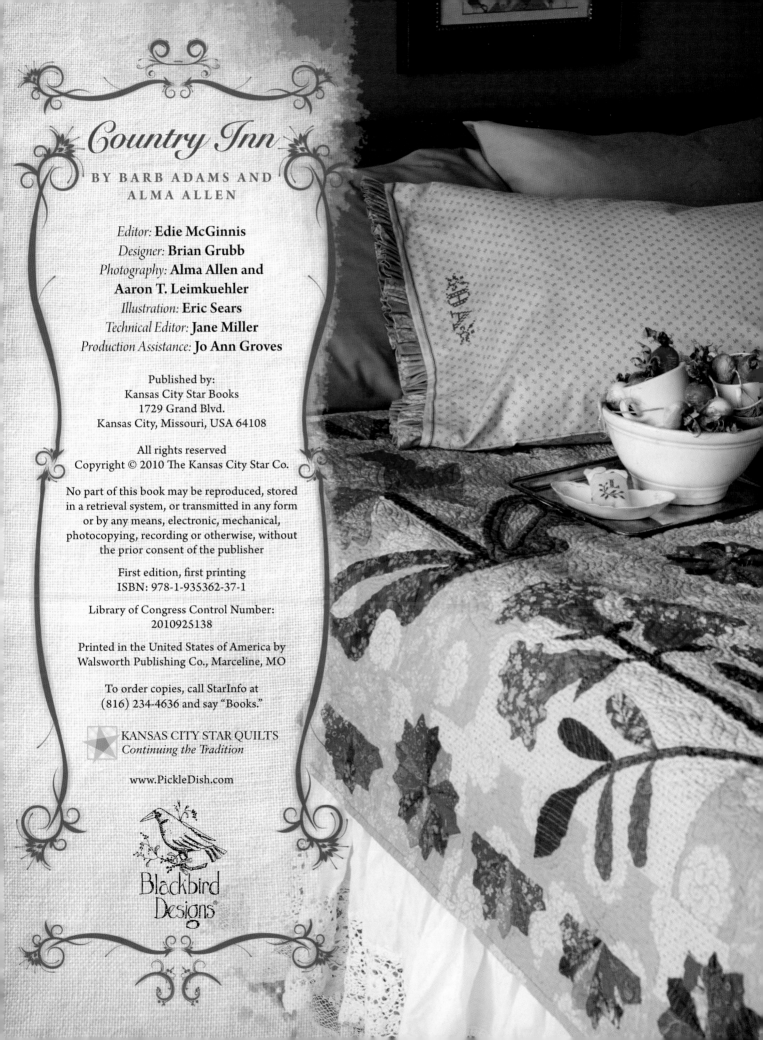

Country Inn

BY BARB ADAMS AND ALMA ALLEN

Editor: **Edie McGinnis**
Designer: **Brian Grubb**
Photography: **Alma Allen and Aaron T. Leimkuehler**
Illustration: **Eric Sears**
Technical Editor: **Jane Miller**
Production Assistance: **Jo Ann Groves**

Published by:
Kansas City Star Books
1729 Grand Blvd.
Kansas City, Missouri, USA 64108

All rights reserved
Copyright © 2010 The Kansas City Star Co.

No part of this book may be reproduced, stored
in a retrieval system, or transmitted in any form
or by any means, electronic, mechanical,
photocopying, recording or otherwise, without
the prior consent of the publisher

First edition, first printing
ISBN: 978-1-935362-37-1

Library of Congress Control Number:
2010925138

Printed in the United States of America by
Walsworth Publishing Co., Marceline, MO

To order copies, call StarInfo at
(816) 234-4636 and say "Books."

KANSAS CITY STAR QUILTS
Continuing the Tradition

www.PickleDish.com

Blackbird
Designs®

Acknowledgements

This book would not have been possible without the contributions of many.

The quilting of Jeanne Zyck and Brenda Butcher added design and texture to our pieces that reflect and enhance our patterns. It's never a quilt until it's quilted and these women certainly know their craft.

We love the fun use of the Moda pre-cuts in Jeanne Zyck's quilt. Her design has a sense of fun and ease. It's a perfect quilt to make when welcoming a new baby.

Many hours of time must be devoted to bring projects to completion. The sewing skills of Leona Adams are essential to this endeavor.

My friend and editor, Edie McGinnis went with me to Country Sampler in Spring Green, Wisconsin. We traveled through snow-covered roads to cook and photograph the food. The recipes she shared added much flavor to this book. Her inspiration gave focus to the idea of Anna and Henry, the cook and gardener of Blackbird's Country Inn. Where would we be without our friends?

Our photographer, Aaron Leimkuehler, has captured the beauty of our projects and quilts through the eye of the camera. It's always a pleasure to work on a project with Aaron.

The illustrating talent of Eric Sears is essential to this project. His understanding of the quilting process and drawing skills brings clarity to the instructions.

Alissa Christianson graphs our cross stitch patterns. There is a real artistry in using the symbols to shade the design, making it easy to count and stitch.

The beautiful book design by Brian Grubb binds our efforts into a compelling format. His vision of the book illuminates our theme. His assistance during the photography of the projects offered a new and welcomed perspective.

Photographs must be color corrected for printing and Jo Ann Groves accomplishes this magic. Any loose threads or problems are digitally corrected by Jo Ann.

No one wants mistakes in their quilting books. Jane Miller shares her mathematical ability as she goes over each and every pattern to make sure there is enough fabric, the correct number of pieces are cut and we are consistent and accurate with our instructions. Believe me, everyone thanks you, Jane!

Thanks to all of you for your continued support and kindness. We hope this book will bring you inspiration and hours of pleasure.

Menu

Manoir d Bras, le 14 Octobre 1922

Introduction

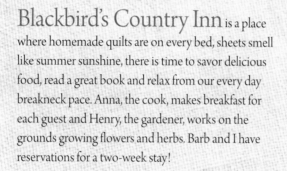

Blackbird's Country Inn is a place where homemade quilts are on every bed, sheets smell like summer sunshine, there is time to savor delicious food, read a great book and relax from our every day breakneck pace. Anna, the cook, makes breakfast for each guest and Henry, the gardener, works on the grounds growing flowers and herbs. Barb and I have reservations for a two-week stay!

As Barb and I began to imagine this idyllic place, we thought about bringing this feeling of comfort into our own homes. Everyone wants their guests to feel pampered and loved. So before your friends and family arrive, tuck some sachets into a basket, cover the beds with quilts and let them wake up to a special breakfast made from the recipes in this book.

Take a break from your daily routine and experiment with trims and buttons as you make *Lavender Sachets*. Spend an afternoon antiquing and pick up some vintage glass containers. Using your finds, try our easy candle making instructions and make your own *Vintage Tea Lights*.

An old frame can come to life with a cork board and some fabric hexagons. *Hexagon Pin Board* is a perfect place to leave notes to your guests and provide a place for them to hang their small items during their visit. The *Country Charm* quilt is just the right size to provide a bit of extra warmth your guest might need in the evening while visiting out on the porch.

Our featured quilts, *Evening Bloom* and *Country Rose,* are sure to leave your guest room at its best. Our favorite garden flowers blossom on each of the nine large blocks. The large shapes of each of the flowers are easy to appliqué. Different color and border options are provided for the two quilts. Barb's *Evening Bloom* uses red and grey tones. It makes an elegant statement. Her border treatment continues the circular motion of the fan block. Mine, *Country Rose,* uses the spring and summer shades of pink and green. A feminine scalloped border frames the garden.

We welcome you to Blackbird's Country Inn. Stay as long as you like. When you are here with us, your appliqué stitches don't have to be perfect and all your points don't have to match! It's the fun and laughter of friendship we like best.

– Alma Allen

Hand Appliqué Instructions

❋ Make templates of the appliqué shapes using freezer paper or plastic template material. Do not add any seam allowance to these shapes.

❋ If using plastic, trace around the templates on the right side of your fabric. Use a marking pencil that will be easy to see on your fabric. This drawn line indicates your seam line. To cut reversed pieces, flip the plastic template over and trace the reversed shape to the right side of the fabric. If using freezer paper, first trace the shapes onto the dull side of the paper. Iron the paper templates, shiny side down, onto the right side of the fabric. Trace around the template. Peel the paper template away carefully, as it can be reused. For a reversed piece, trace on the shiny side of the paper.

❋ After the seam line has been drawn on the right side of the fabric, cut out the shapes, adding a 1/8" - 1/4" seam allowance.

❋ Fold the background fabric in half vertically and horizontally. Finger press the folds. Open the fabric.

❋ To help achieve placement of the design, refer to the block diagram located with the templates. A one-inch grid was added to each diagram to indicate position for the pieces. If you look closely at each quilt block, you will notice each is unique. The pieces were placed on the block in a whimsical fashion.

❋ Center the design on the background block using the fold lines and placement diagram as a guide.

❋ Baste the shapes into place on the background block with glue stick or appliqué pins. Larger shapes require basting stitches to hold the shapes in place securely.

❋ Use thread that matches your appliqué piece, not the background. Use a two-ply, cotton thread that is 50-60 weight.

❋ Cut the thread length about 12" - 15". Longer lengths of thread may become worn and break as you stitch.

❋ For concave curves (curves that go in) clip to the seam line, then turn under the seam allowance. This will allow the fabric to lie flat. Convex curves (or curves that go out) do not require clipping.

❋ Sew the pieces that will be covered by another piece first. For example, sew the stems first. Next, sew the flower or leaf that covers the end of the stem.

❋ Using the point and edge of your needle, turn under the fabric on the drawn seam line and appliqué the shape to the background fabric. Try to achieve about 7-9 stitches per inch.

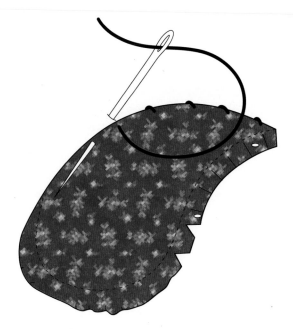

APPLIQUÉ STITCH

Supply List

EVENING BLOOM

PROJECT SIZE - 80" X 80"

FINISHED BLOCK SIZE - 24"

Fabrics from collections of *Rouenneries* by the French General for Moda Fabrics and *Worn and Loved* series by Jeanne Horton for Windham Fabrics

FOR BACKGROUNDS

4 2/3 yds. gray and tan motif print
   (including binding)
1 3/4 yds. gray and tan floral print
1 1/4 yds. tan and gray geometric print

FOR APPLIQUE PIECES

1/2 yd. each of 4 different red prints
1/4 yd. pink print
1/4 yd. red and white print
1/2 yd. each of 5 different dark gray and tan prints
1/4 yd. each of 3 different dark gray and tan prints and wovens

1/2" Clover bias tape maker
3/4" Clover bias tape maker

COUNTRY ROSE

PROJECT SIZE - 88" X 88"

FINISHED BLOCK SIZE - 24"

Reference numbers *Garden Party* by Blackbird Designs for Moda fabrics are provided below:

FOR BACKGROUNDS

3 1/2 yds. cream - large floral print for the border and sashing (2650-16)

2 yds. cream - small daisy floral print for the blocks, sashing and binding (2653-16)

1 yd. cream - small petunia floral print for the blocks and sashing (2652-16)

1 1/2 yds. cream - small bird floral print for the blocks and sashing (2651-16)

1 yd. cream - small leaves print for the blocks and sashing (2655-12)

FOR APPLIQUE PIECES

1/3 yd. rose blush - small dot print (2656-12)
1/3 yd. rose blush - sampler print (2658-22)
1/4 yd. rose blush - lattice print (2654-12)
1/3 yd. rose blush - small daisy print (2653-12)
1/3 yd. rose blush - small bird print (2651-12)
1/3 yd. rose blush - small check (2657-12)
1/2 yd. each of 4 different green prints
1/3 yd. each of 2 different green prints

1/2" Clover bias tape maker
3/4" Clover bias tape maker

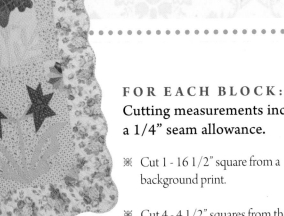

FOR EACH BLOCK:

Cutting measurements include a 1/4" seam allowance.

※ Cut 1 - 16 1/2" square from a background print.

※ Cut 4 - 4 1/2" squares from the same background print for the corner units.

※ Cut 4 - 4 1/2" x 16 1/2" rectangles from a different background print for the sashing.

※ Cut 12 diamonds: 8 from one color and 4 from an alternating color for the corner units. Refer to the picture of each block to determine color placement. You will find the template on page 49.

※ Sew 3 diamonds together and appliqué them to a corner unit. Repeat for the remaining 3 corner units.

※ Refer to the diagram below and sew the pieces together to make one block. Make 9 blocks.

Corner unit - 4"

| 16" x 4" |
| 4" x 16"   16" x 16"   4" x 16" |
| 16" x 4" |

Background block - 24" finished

Strawberry Jam

ach morning a delicious offering is prepared for the guests at Blackbird's Country Inn.

In the cook's garden, strawberries are grown and harvested each spring. The freshest, ripest strawberries are picked to make enough strawberry jam to last throughout the year. The jars of jam are stored in the freezer and thawed as needed. The bright, intense color and fresh flavor of the berries is always a welcome addition to the breakfast table.

Every fall, Henry the gardener, faithfully adds the cook's favorite pink tulip bulbs to the flower beds. He remembers her shy smile as he tucks each bulb into the ground.

When the blooms begin to open in the spring, he cuts a dozen tulips just for her. The cook, looking at this generous man, in turn, tucks a jar of jam into his jacket pocket for his morning toast.

Strawberry Jam

2 cups (about 1 quart) strawberries – washed, stemmed and crushed
4 cups sugar
3/4 cup water
1 box Sure-Jell fruit pectin

Before you begin: Wash the jars in the dishwasher. Allow the jars to go through the complete cycle. Dip the jars in boiling water. Wash and rinse the jar lids and dip in boiling water.

INSTRUCTIONS

Measure and put the crushed berries into a large bowl.

Thoroughly mix the sugar into the prepared fruit and let stand for 10 minutes.

Mix the water and fruit pectin in a small saucepan. Bring the mixture to a full boil. Boil for 1 minute, stirring constantly. Remove from heat.

Add the water/pectin mixture to the fruit. Stir constantly for 3 more minutes, until the sugar is dissolved. (A few sugar crystals will remain.)

Ladle the mixture quickly into the prepared containers, filling to within 1/2" of tops. Wipe the top edge of the jar to remove any jam. Cover at once with the lids. Let the jars stand at room temperature for 24 hours for the jam to set, then store in the freezer.

Yield: about 4 3/4 cups

The Tulip Block
BLOCK 1

COUNTRY ROSE

❋ Locate the placement diagram on page 50. Note the templates needed for this block. The templates are located on pages 50 - 52. Refer to the photo for color placement.

❋ Make 16" of 3/4" bias tape for the flower stem.

❋ Cut out the shapes, adding a 1/8" - 1/4" seam allowance. Refer to the diagram and baste the pieces in place on the background block.

❋ Appliqué the pieces to the background.

Stuffed French Toast

A nna, the cook at the Blackbird Country Inn, makes this special treat for her guests. The surprise filling in this French toast adds sweetness to each bite. It's the perfect start for those who have plans for non-stop sightseeing or shopping.

Pink petunia plants are picked up from the nursery each spring by Henry. As he tucks each into small decorative pots, he thinks of Anna decorating the table with these blooms later in the morning. The bloom on the trailing stems offers a bit of country sunshine to each table.

Stuffed French Toast

4 - 6 slices of French bread sliced on the diagonal
2 eggs
1/2 cup milk
1/4 teaspoon salt
4 oz. cream cheese
1/4 cup powdered sugar
1/2 teaspoon almond extract or flavoring of your choice

INSTRUCTIONS

Set out the cream cheese to soften. Mix the powdered sugar, almond extract and cream cheese together. Spread the mixture on one side of a piece of bread. Pick up another piece of bread and sandwich the two together. Repeat for all pieces of bread.

Whisk the egg, milk and salt together. Dip a sandwich into the egg mixture. Soak well on both sides. Cook on a well-greased medium hot griddle. Brown one side and flip over to brown the other side. Sprinkle with powdered sugar and add a bit of jam or syrup.

Serves 2 - 3 people

The Petunia Block
BLOCK 2

COUNTRY ROSE

- Locate the placement diagram on page 53. Note the templates needed for this block. The templates are located on pages 53 - 54. Refer to the photo for color placement.

- Make 16" of 3/4" bias tape for the flower stem and 28" of 1/2" bias tape for the 2 leaf stems.

- Cut out the shapes, adding a 1/8" - 1/4" seam allowance. Refer to the diagram and baste the pieces in place on the background block.

- Appliqué the pieces to the background.

Date and Walnut Scones

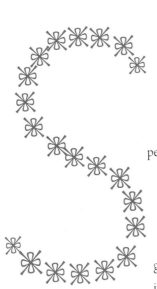

S pending the night at grandmother's house was always fun for Anna when she was a child. She would carry a basket of fresh baked scones out into the garden as her grandmother spread a blanket on the ground. Eating her scone with delight, she would watch her Grandmother cut peony blooms for bouquets.

Anna still uses her grandmother's recipe when she bakes these rich tea biscuits for the guests at Blackbird's Country Inn. Henry seems to time his arrival to the kitchen door just as she takes them out of the oven.

Date and Walnut Scones

2 cups all-purpose flour
1/4 cup sugar
1 tablespoon baking powder
1/2 teaspoon salt
2 teaspoons orange zest
6 tablespoons cold unsalted butter (cut into 1/2" pieces)
1/2 cup finely chopped dates
1/4 cup finely chopped walnuts
3/4 cup heavy cream

FOR THE TOPPING:

Vanilla sugar
2 teaspoons heavy cream

INSTRUCTIONS

In a large bowl, stir together the flour, sugar, baking powder, salt and orange zest. Using a pastry blender, cut in the butter until the mixture forms large, coarse crumbs. Add the dates and the walnuts. Pour the cream into the mixture and mix with a rubber spatula just until the ingredients are moistened.

Turn the dough out onto a lightly floured surface and press gently into a ball. Knead 2 - 3 times. Pat the dough out into a circle about 3/4" thick and 6" in diameter. Cut into 6 wedges and place them on a cookie sheet lined with parchment paper.

TO MAKE THE TOPPING:

Brush each scone with the heavy cream. Sprinkle vanilla sugar on top.

Bake at 425 degrees for 13-17 minutes or until golden brown.

Makes 6 scones

The Peony Block
BLOCK 3

❧ Locate the placement diagram on page 55. Note the templates needed for this block. The flower templates are located on pages 55 - 56. The leaf template is on page 52. Refer to the photo for color placement.

❧ Make 16" of 3/4" bias tape for the flower stem.

❧ Cut out the shapes, adding a 1/8" - 1/4" seam allowance. Refer to the diagram and baste the pieces in place on the background block.

❧ Appliqué the pieces to the background.

Sausage and Egg Casserole

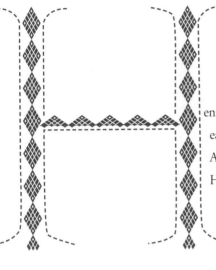

enry loves working outside in the garden. The smell of the earth and the feel of the wind on his skin is a sensual delight. As he begins his day he takes a few minutes to stretch out his back. He's reminded that he's not as young as he used to be.

Suddenly out of the corner of his eye, he spots two small fox pups playing on the eastern hillside slope by the perennial garden. He knows Anna is up early working in the kitchen and she will want to know about them. Every year they eagerly watch for a new litter of pups. Watching their antics is one of their favorite events in the spring and early summer.

Sausage and Egg Casserole

6 eggs
1 cup milk
1 teaspoon ground mustard
1/2 teaspoon salt
1/2 pound mild ground pork sausage (cooked and drained)
1 cup shredded cheddar cheese
1 cup cubed white bread

INSTRUCTIONS

In a large bowl, whisk the eggs, milk, mustard and salt together. Stir in the sausage, cheese and bread cubes. Use 6 custard cups or pour into a greased 8" x 9" x 2" baking dish. Cover and refrigerate overnight.

Remove from the refrigerator 30 minutes before baking. Bake uncovered at 350 degrees for 30 minutes or until a knife inserted near the center comes out clean. Let stand for 10 minutes before serving.

Serves 6

The Foxglove Block
BLOCK 4

COUNTRY ROSE

* Locate the placement diagram and templates on page 57. Note the templates needed for this block. The templates for the leaves is on pages 53 – 54. Refer to the photo for color placement.

* Make 16" of 3/4" bias tape for the flower stem and 28" of 1/2" bias tape for the 2 leaf stems.

* Cut out the shapes, adding a 1/8" - 1/4" seam allowance. Refer to the diagram and baste the pieces in place on the background block.

* Appliqué the pieces to the background.

Swedish Pancakes

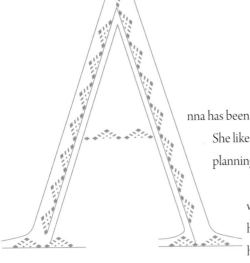

Anna has been the cook at Blackbird's Country Inn for years. The job suits her. She likes the freedom of running this large comfortable kitchen and planning the menus.

She always finds time to chat with the guests. Anna knows many well as they return to the Inn year after year. She doesn't mind sharing her recipies and has found some of the guests have shared some with her too. The Swedish Pancake recipe is from her friend Jeannie who introduced her to Lingonberries.

Swedish Pancakes

4 eggs
1 2/3 cup milk
1 cup flour
3/4 teaspoon salt
1 1/2 tablespoons sugar

INSTRUCTIONS

Put all ingredients into a blender and blend until smooth. The batter will be very thin. Pour into the buttered wells of a hot Dollar Pancake Griddle.* If you don't have a Dollar Pancake griddle, pour out onto a buttered griddle in small circles.

Butter the pancakes and spread with lingonberries. Pour maple syrup over all.

Serves 8

*The Dollar Pancake Griddle can be found at
 Harry and David.
 http://www.harryanddavid.com

The Iris Block
BLOCK 5

COUNTRY ROSE

* Locate the placement diagram and templates on page 58. Note the templates needed for this block. The leaf template is on page 52. Refer to the photo for color placement.

* Make 16" of 3/4" bias tape for the flower stem.

* Cut out the shapes, adding a 1/8" - 1/4" seam allowance. Refer to the diagram and baste the pieces in place on the background block.

* Appliqué the pieces to the background.

Broiled Grapefruit

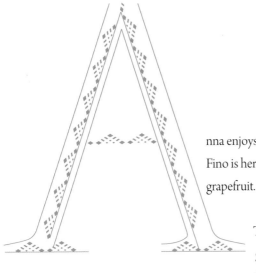

Anna enjoys the savory flavor of adding a bit of sherry to some of her dishes. Fino is her favorite to add to soups and stews. She even adds a splash on her grapefruit. The pale gold color, with a delicate crisp aroma is its hallmark.

During the winter, she adds this recipe to her Sunday brunch. The guests at Blackbird's Country Inn are usually surprised at the great taste. Many tell her they will try this easy recipe again when they return home.

Broiled Grapefruit

1 grapefruit
2 tablespoons of sugar
Splash of sherry

INSTRUCTIONS

Cut 1 grapefruit in half. Trim the bottom a small amount so the grapefruit will sit flat in the baking dish. Sprinkle at least 1 tablespoon of sugar over each half. Broil until the grapefruit is warm. Splash a bit of sherry over each half.

Serves 2

The Coxcomb Block
BLOCK 6

❧ Locate the placement diagram on page 59. Note the templates needed for this block. The flower templates are located on pages 59 - 60. The templates for the leaves are on pages 53 - 54. Refer to the photo for color placement.

❧ Make 16" of 3/4" bias tape for the flower

stem and 28" of 1/2" bias tape for the 2 leaf stems.

❧ Cut out the shapes, adding a 1/8" - 1/4" seam allowance. Refer to the diagram and baste the pieces in place on the background block.

❧ Appliqué the pieces to the background.

Cranberry Orange Muffins

The Inn has been full of guests. Between the laundry, cleaning, cooking and gardening there hasn't been time for the staff to take a break. Anna doesn't mind though. She is at her best during these busy times with lots of food to cook and people to feed.

Even with all of the business, the early morning hours are quiet and calm in her kitchen. As she pulls out the last batch of muffins from the hot oven she looks through the window. Henry is walking into the garden. His unhurried calm manner is a reflection of her own.

He has been spending a bit of time weeding her cook's garden. The basil, parsley, lavender and rosemary are her favorites. She dries leaves of basil all summer and bags the crushed leaves to add to her salads, pastas and pizza during the rest of the year. She uses many herbs in her cooking but she loves of the robust flavor of basil best.

Henry stands and walks toward the kitchen door carrying a sprig of rosemary as Anna carefully places a muffin on a clean white plate and pours him a glass of milk. His easy smile is her greeting for the day.

Cranberry Orange Muffins

3 1/2 cups unbleached all-purpose flour
4 teaspoons baking powder
1/2 teaspoon baking soda
1/2 teaspoon salt
1 1/3 cups sugar
10 tablespoons unsalted butter, melted and slightly cooled
1 cup whole milk
1 cup sour cream
2 large eggs
1 egg yolk
2 teaspoons finely grated orange zest
1 1/2 cups fresh cranberries, coarsley chopped
3/4 cup pecan pieces, toasted

INSTRUCTIONS

Pour the wet ingredients into the dry and fold gently with a rubber spatula until the dry ingredients are moistened. The batter will be lumpy and there will be streaks of flour. Add the orange zest, cranberries, and pecans to the batter. Fold them into the mix until just combined. Do not overmix.

Divide the batter among the muffin cups. The batter should mound higher than the rim of the cups by 3/4". Bake until the muffins are golden brown and spring back lightly when you press the middle, about 30-35 minutes. Allow to cool before adding the glaze. Remove the muffins and place on a rack over a sheet of parchment paper.

FOR THE GLAZE:

Whisk the confectioner's sugar and orange juice together until smooth. The glaze should be thick enough to drip off a spoon. Thin with more orange juice if needed. Spoon the glaze over the muffins and let it drip over the sides. Wait for the glaze to set, then serve. They are best when served the day they are made.

Makes 12 muffins

The Daffodil Block
BLOCK 7

✤ Locate the placement diagram on page 61. Note the templates needed for this block. The flower templates are located on pages 61 – 62. The leaf template is on page 52. Refer to the photo for color placement

✤ Make 16" of 3/4" bias tape for the flower stem.

✤ Cut out the shapes, adding a 1/8" - 1/4" seam allowance. Refer to the diagram and baste the pieces in place on the background block.

✤ Appliqué the pieces to the background.

Laura Renner's Apple Roll-ups

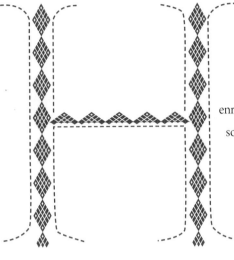

enry has been ill for the past week. Anna has gone by to see him daily bringing soups and other treats for him to eat.

Henry doesn't like being confined to the house. He's not the complaining type, he just likes being outside and free. Just when he's beginning to feel a bit low, a ray of brightness enters his day as Anna shows up with his favorite Apple Roll-ups. She knows his mom used to make them for him when he was little. His eyes fill with tears as he thinks of this woman's kindness to him.

Tucked into a fold of newsprint are bright coneflower blooms to cheer him up. These blooms are as upright and honest as this man she cares for.

Laura Renner's Apple Roll-ups

2 apples
Pillsbury Refrigerated Pie Crust
1/2 cup melted butter
1/2 cup sugar
1/2 cup water
1 teaspoon cinnamon

INSTRUCTIONS

Peel and core the apples. Slice each apple into 8 wedges. Cut the pie crust into 2-inch strips. Wrap a piece of dough around each apple wedge.

Arrange the apple wedges in a 9 x 13 inch baking pan, making sure the pastries don't touch each other or the sides of the pan. Brush them with melted butter. Mix the sugar and cinnamon together and sprinkle over the wedges. Pour 1/2 cup water over the pastries. Bake in a 425 degree oven for 25-30 minutes or until golden brown.

Serve them warm or cold. Henry likes a bit of ice cream with his.

The Coneflower Block
BLOCK 8

COUNTRY ROSE

- Locate the placement diagram and templates on page 63. Note the templates needed for this block. The templates for the leaves are on pages 53 - 54. Refer to the photo for color placement.

- Make 16" of 3/4" bias tape for the flower stem and 28" of 1/2" bias tape for the 2 leaf stems.

- Cut out the shapes, adding a 1/8" - 1/4" seam allowance. Refer to the diagram and baste the pieces in place on the background block.

- Appliqué the pieces to the background.

Belgian Waffle Bits

When waffles are on the menu, Anna needs help in the kitchen. Her friend Lizzie, the upstairs housekeeper, comes to her aid. Anna places Lizzie in charge of the waffle irons. These waffles are a Country Inn favorite.

Lizzie is good natured and always willing to help in the kitchen. She has a habit of humming as she pours the mixture into the waffle irons. Anna's even seen Lizzie pop a waffle bit in her mouth as she works but she will never scold her. She's done the same thing herself.

Belgian Waffle Bits

1 package dried yeast
1/3 cup lukewarm water
1 1/2 tablespoons granulated sugar
1/8 teaspoon salt
2 cups flour
3 eggs
1 cup softened butter
1 cup Demerara sugar (or pearl sugar if you can find it)

INSTRUCTIONS

Mix the yeast, water, sugar and salt in a bowl and let develop for 15 minutes.

Place the flour into a large bowl. Make a well in the flour, pour in the yeast mixture and stir. Add the eggs, one at a time. Add the butter, 2 tablespoons at a time, mixing well.

Let the dough rest in the bowl until it's doubled.

Gently mix in the Demerara sugar. Let the dough rest for 15 minutes.

Heat a waffle iron. When it's hot, butter the waffle iron and pour in 2-3 tablespoons of dough per waffle. Cook for 3-5 minutes, until the waffle is lightly browned. Serve warm with a bit of syrup.

The Daylily Block
BLOCK 9

❧ Locate the placement diagram on page 64. Note the templates needed for this block. The flower templates are located on pages 64 - 65. The leaf template is on page 52. Refer to the photo for color placement.

❧ Make 16" of 3/4" bias tape for the flower stem.

❧ Cut out the shapes, adding a 1/8" - 1/4" seam allowance. Refer to the diagram and baste the pieces in place on the background block.

❧ Appliqué the pieces to the background.

TEMPLATES FOR
EVENING BLOOM AND
COUNTRY ROSE

CUT THE TEMPLATE OUT USING FREEZER PAPER. DO NOT ADD A SEAM ALLOWANCE TO THE FREEZER PAPER. IRON THE PAPER TO THE REVERSE SIDE OF THE FABRIC. CUT THE DIAMOND OUT, ADDING A 1/4" SEAM ALLOWANCE. SEW THREE TOGETHER AND APPLIQUÉ IN PLACE ONTO THE CORNER SQUARE.

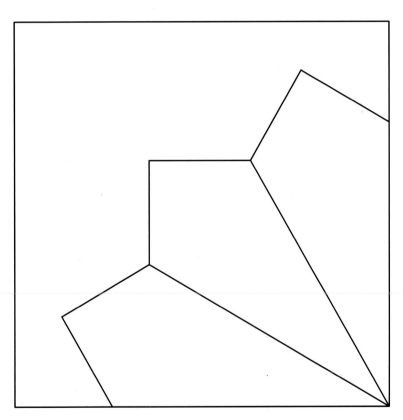

Corner unit of the block

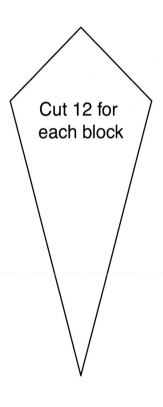

Cut 12 for each block

DIAMOND TEMPLATES FOR THE CORNER UNIT

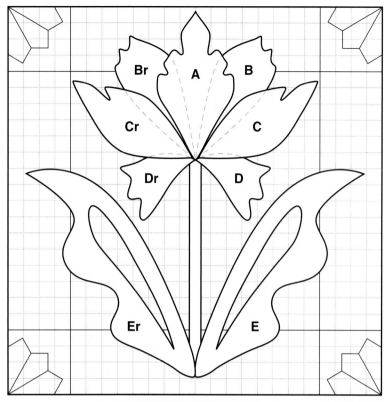

One square = 1"

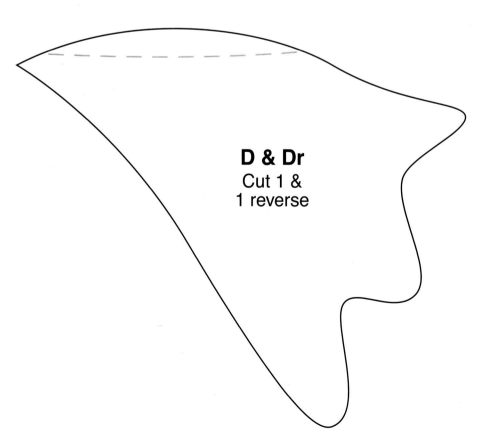

D & Dr
Cut 1 &
1 reverse

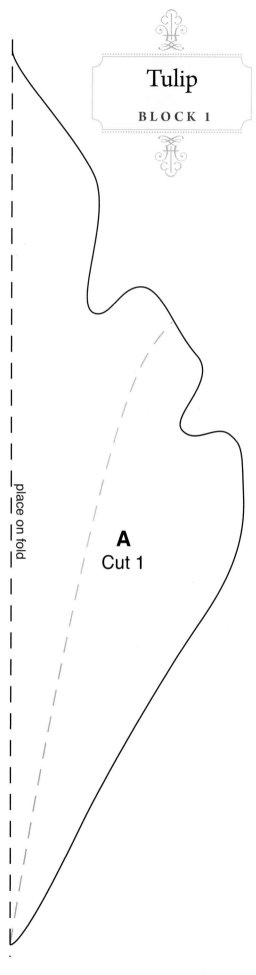

place on fold

A
Cut 1

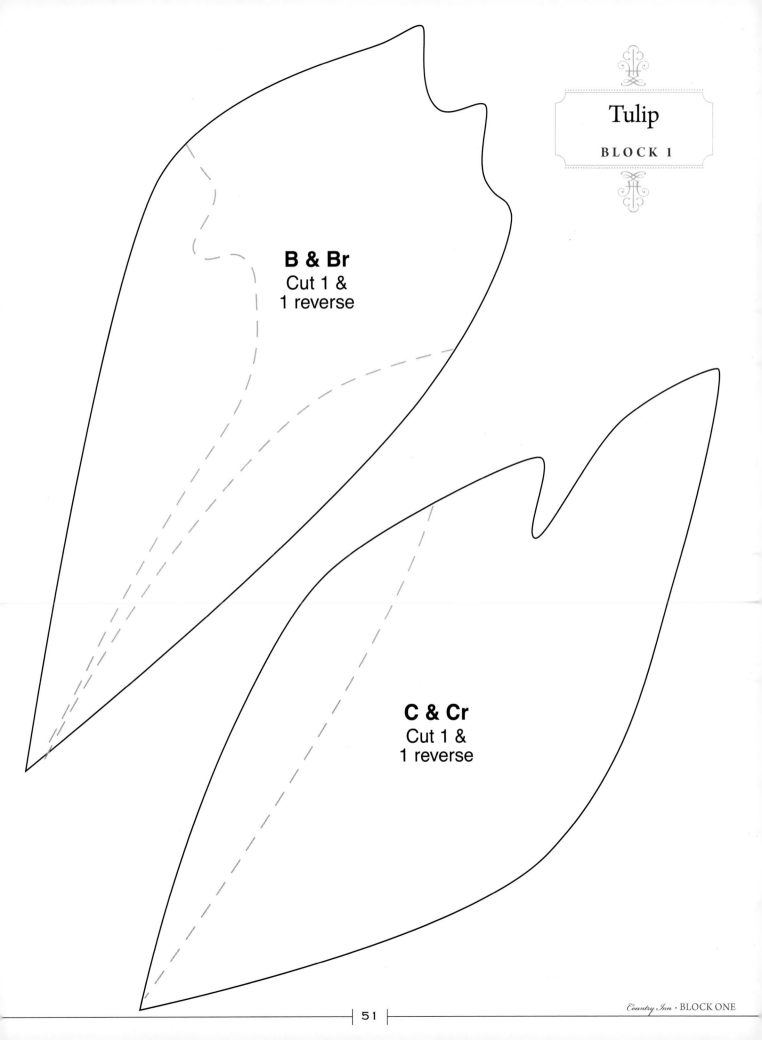

Tulip

BLOCK 1

B & Br
Cut 1 &
1 reverse

C & Cr
Cut 1 &
1 reverse

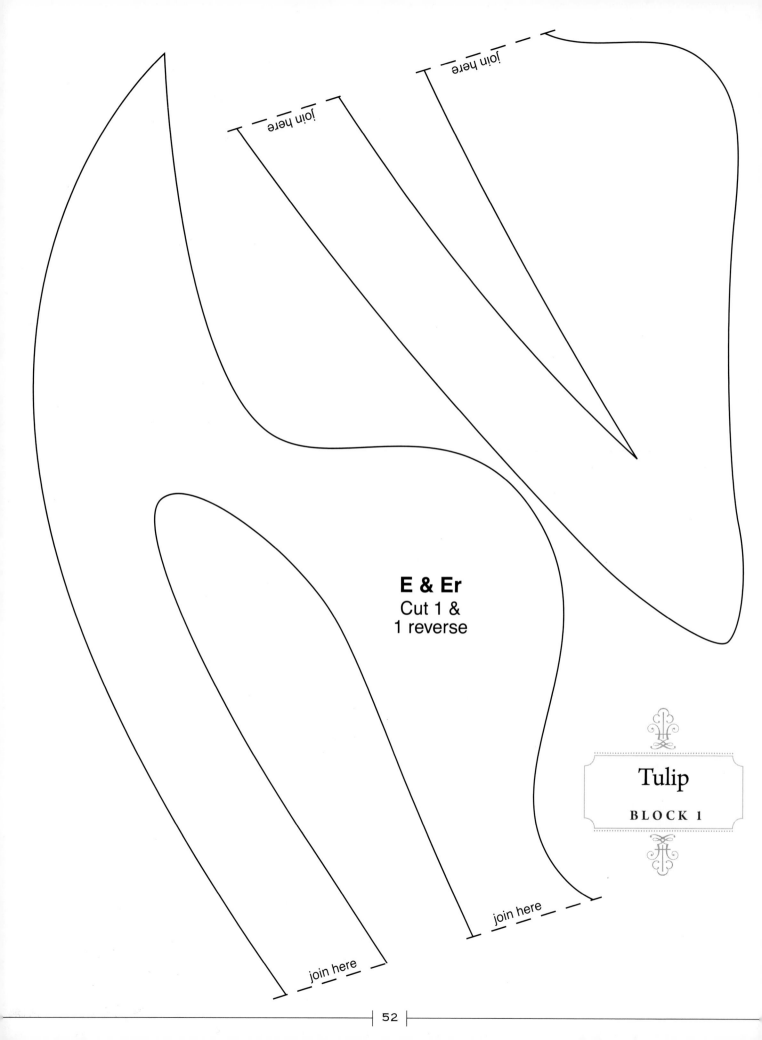

join here

join here

E & Er
Cut 1 &
1 reverse

join here

Tulip

BLOCK 1

join here

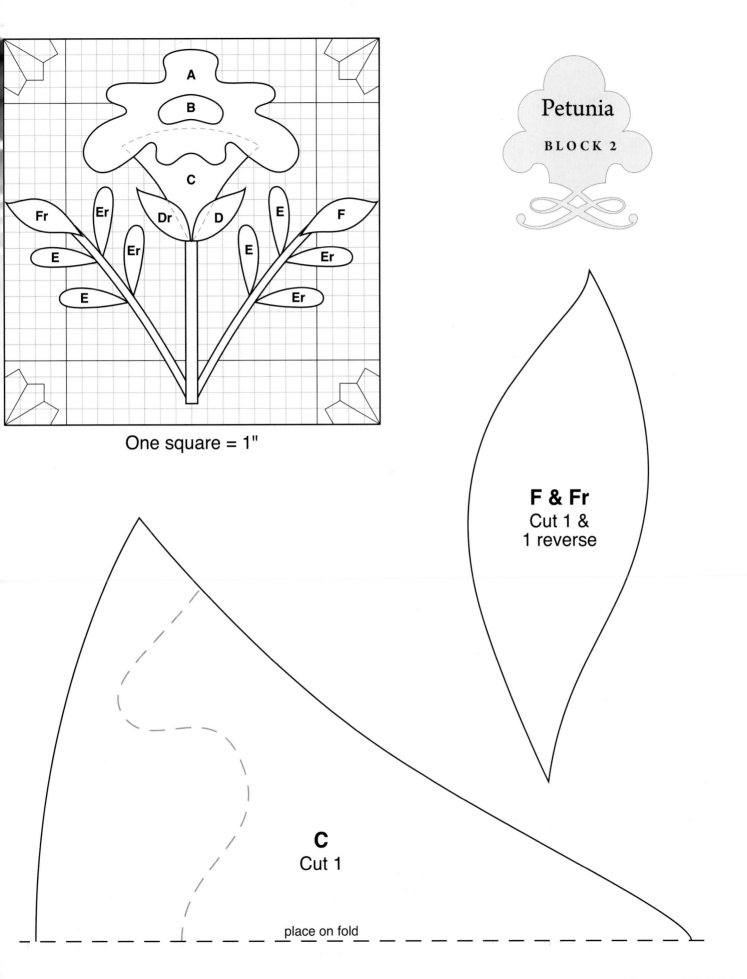

One square = 1"

Petunia

BLOCK 2

F & Fr
Cut 1 &
1 reverse

C
Cut 1

place on fold

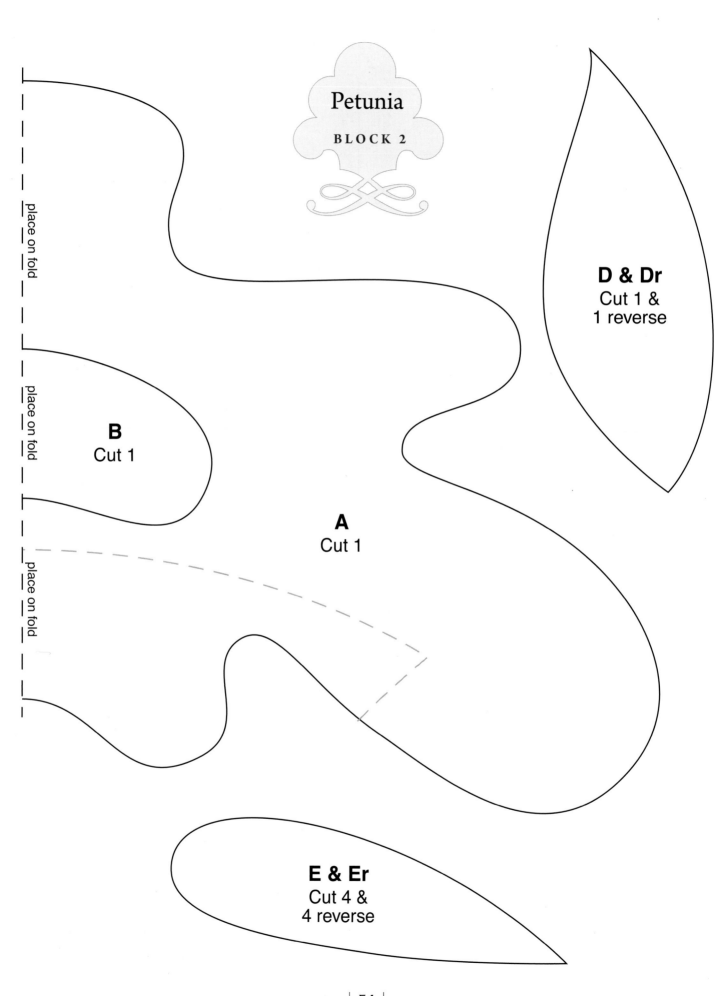

Petunia

BLOCK 2

D & Dr
Cut 1 &
1 reverse

place on fold

place on fold

place on fold

B
Cut 1

A
Cut 1

E & Er
Cut 4 &
4 reverse

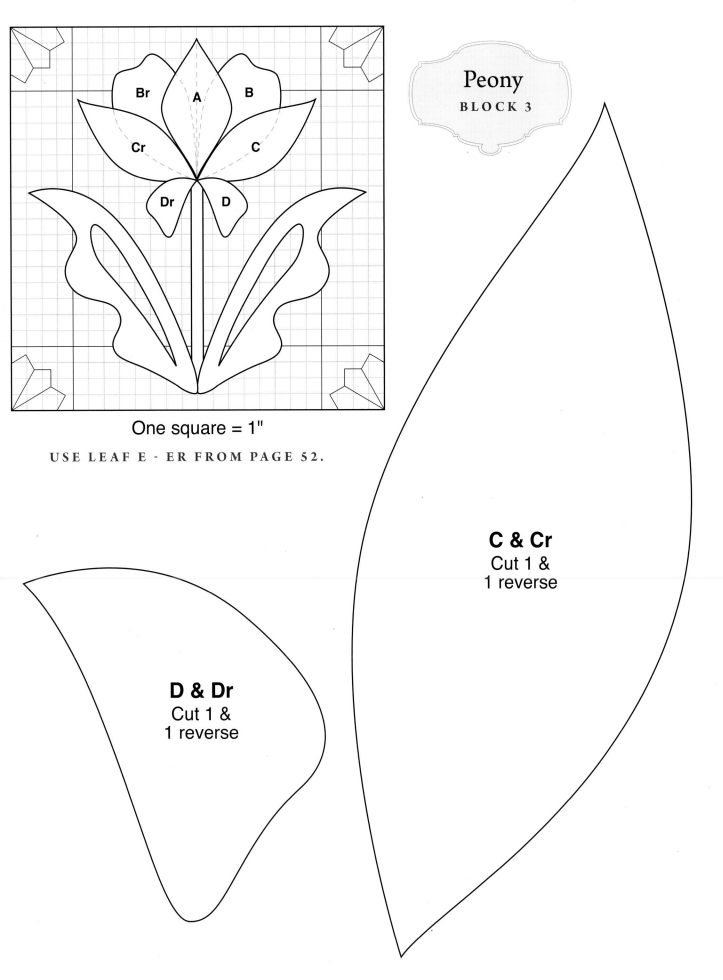

One square = 1"

USE LEAF E - ER FROM PAGE 52.

Peony

BLOCK 3

C & Cr
Cut 1 &
1 reverse

D & Dr
Cut 1 &
1 reverse

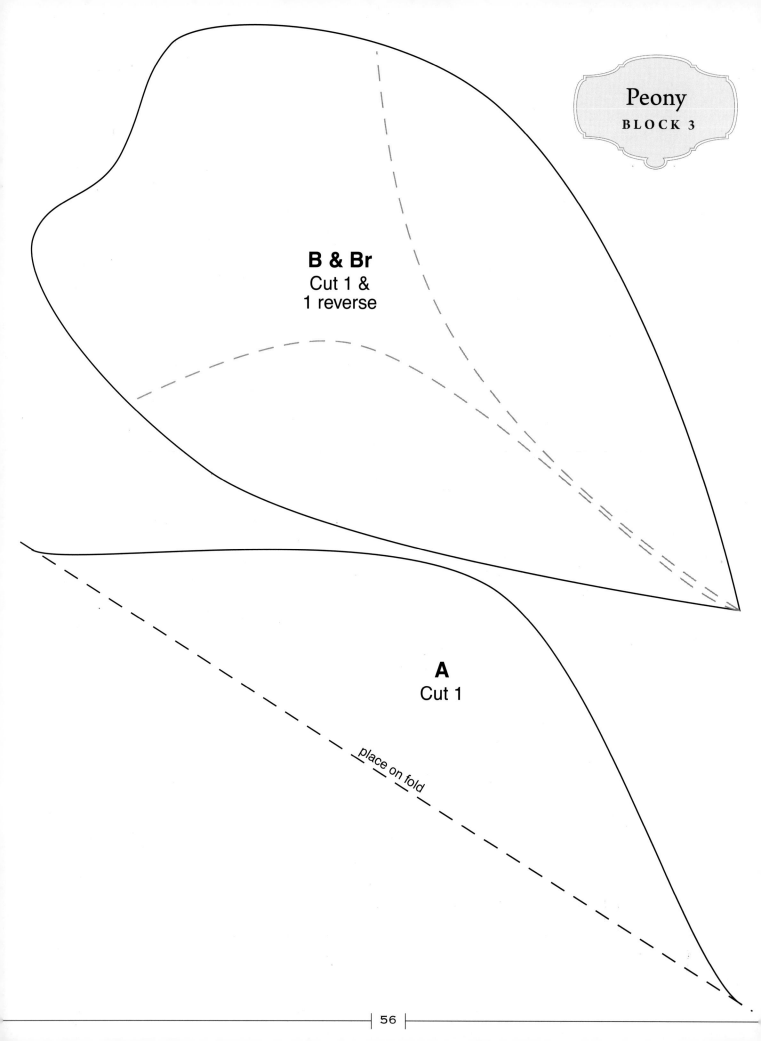

Peony
BLOCK 3

B & Br
Cut 1 &
1 reverse

A
Cut 1

place on fold

One square = 1"

USE THE LEAVES FROM BLOCK 2 LOCATED
ON PAGE 53 - 54.

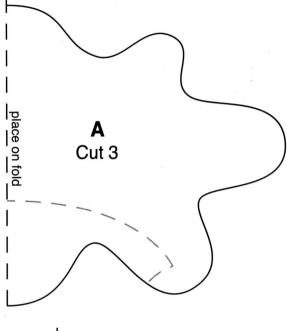

place on fold

A
Cut 3

C & Cr
Cut 1 &
1 reverse

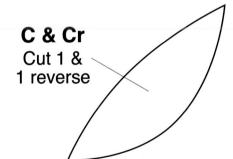

B
Cut 3

place on fold

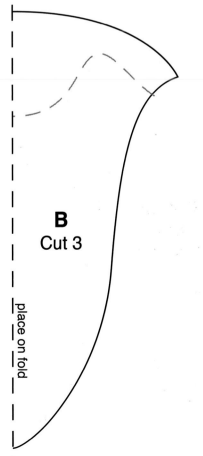

D & Dr
Cut 1 &
1 reverse

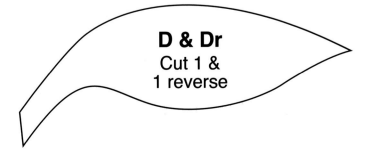

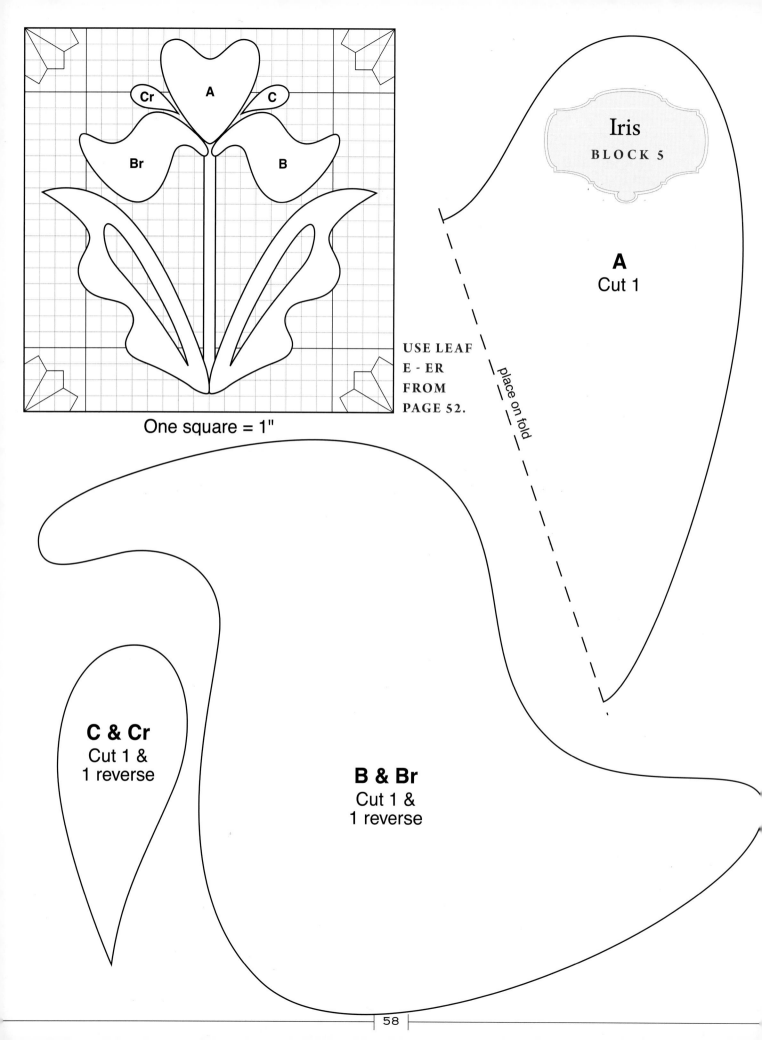

One square = 1"

USE LEAF
E - ER
FROM
PAGE 52.

Cr **A** **C**

Br **B**

Iris
BLOCK 5

A
Cut 1

place on fold

C & Cr
Cut 1 &
1 reverse

B & Br
Cut 1 &
1 reverse

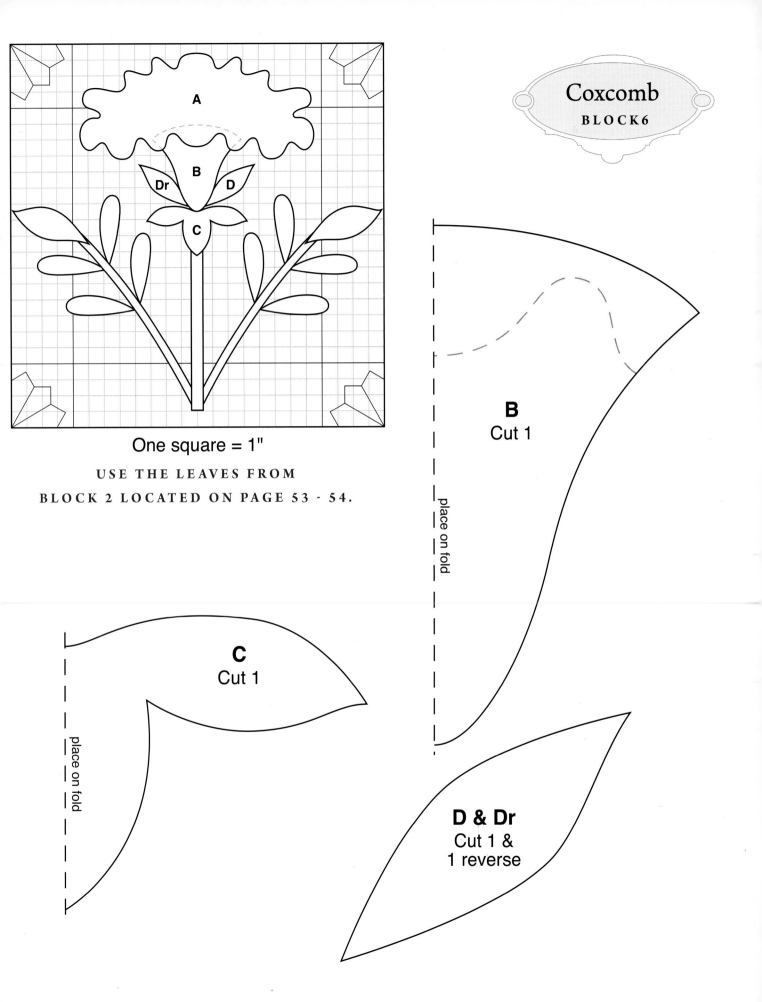

One square = 1"

USE THE LEAVES FROM
BLOCK 2 LOCATED ON PAGE 53 - 54.

Coxcomb
BLOCK 6

B
Cut 1

place on fold

C
Cut 1

place on fold

D & Dr
Cut 1 &
1 reverse

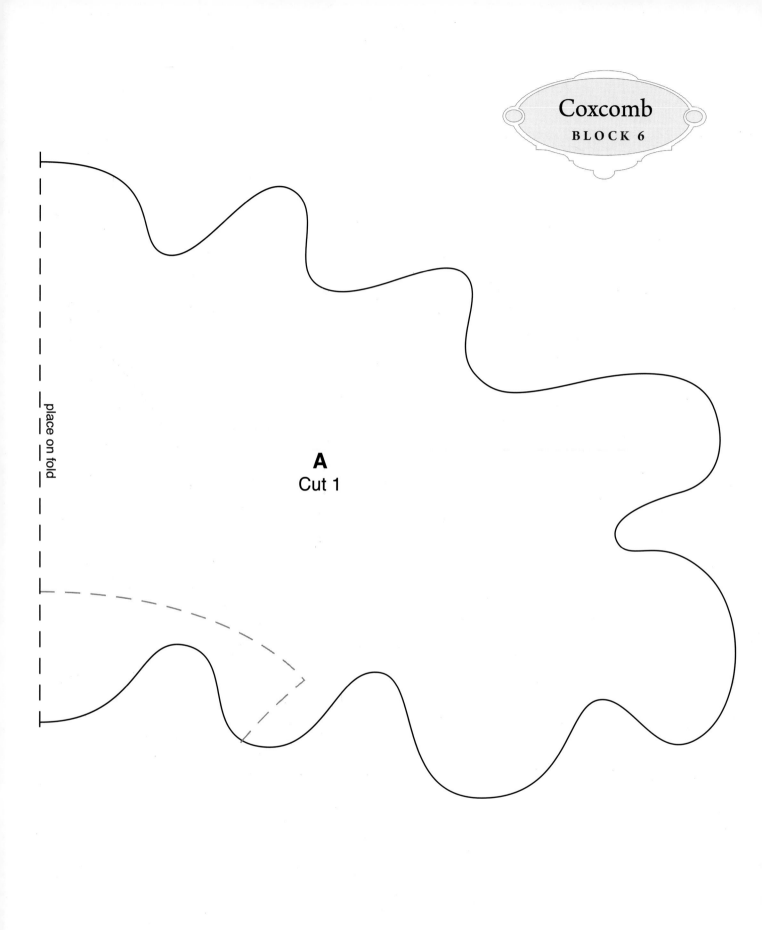

Coxcomb
BLOCK 6

place on fold

A
Cut 1

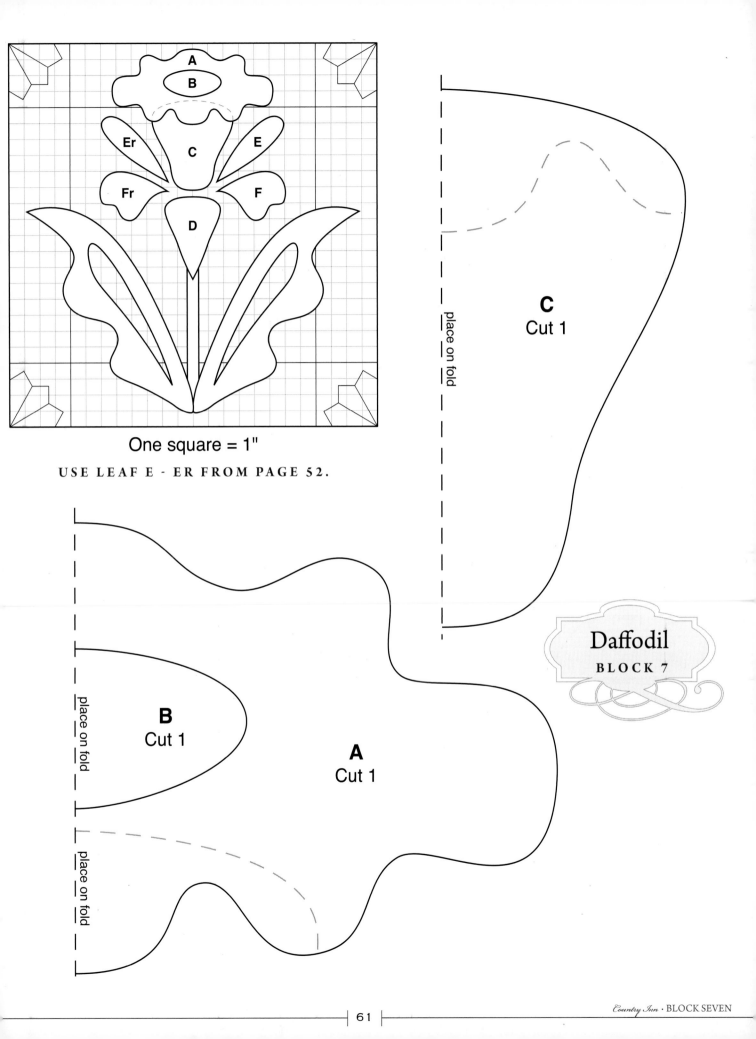

One square = 1"

USE LEAF E - ER FROM PAGE 52.

place on fold

C
Cut 1

place on fold

B
Cut 1

A
Cut 1

place on fold

Daffodil
BLOCK 7

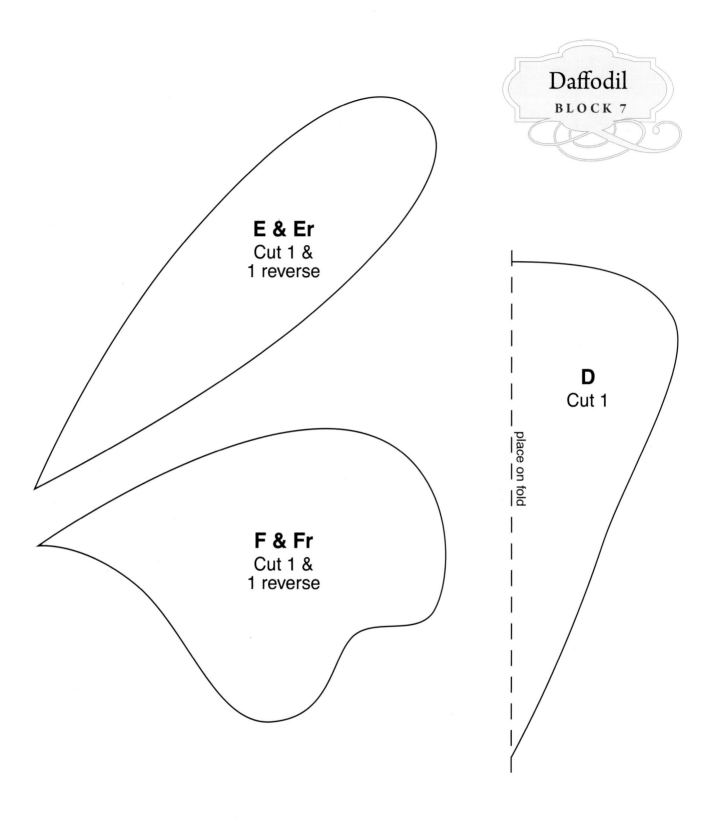

Daffodil

BLOCK 7

E & Er
Cut 1 &
1 reverse

D
Cut 1

place on fold

F & Fr
Cut 1 &
1 reverse

One square = 1"

USE THE LEAVES FROM
BLOCK 2 LOCATED ON PAGE 53 - 54.

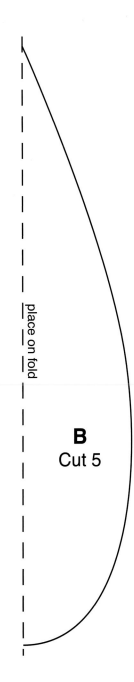

place on fold

B
Cut 5

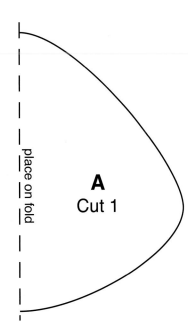

place on fold

A
Cut 1

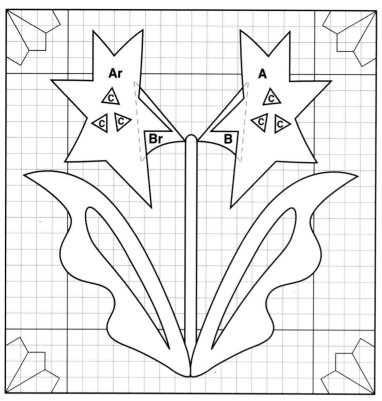

One square = 1"

USE LEAF E - ER LOCATED ON PAGE 52.

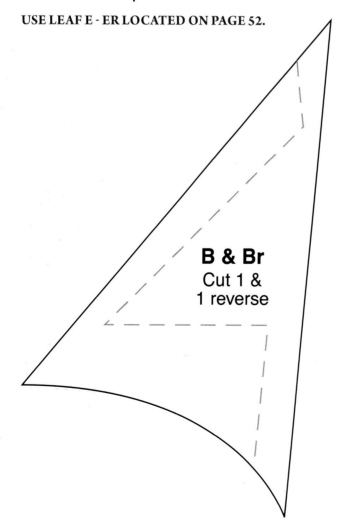

B & Br
Cut 1 &
1 reverse

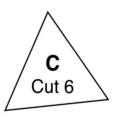

C
Cut 6

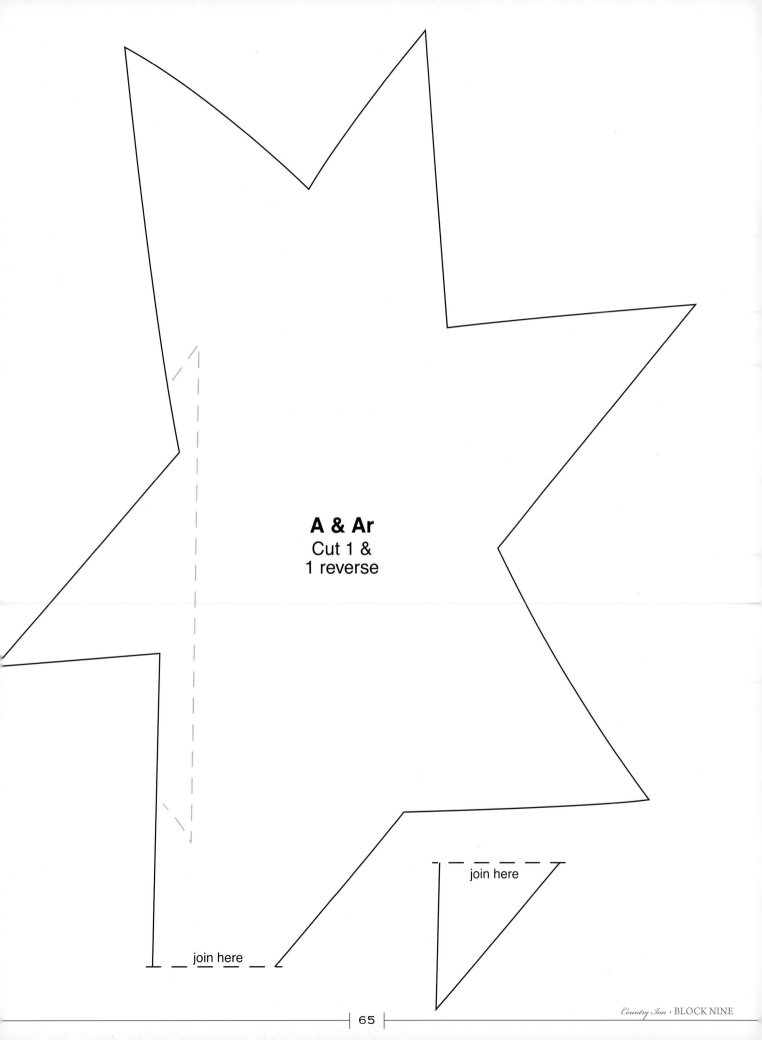

A & Ar
Cut 1 &
1 reverse

join here

join here

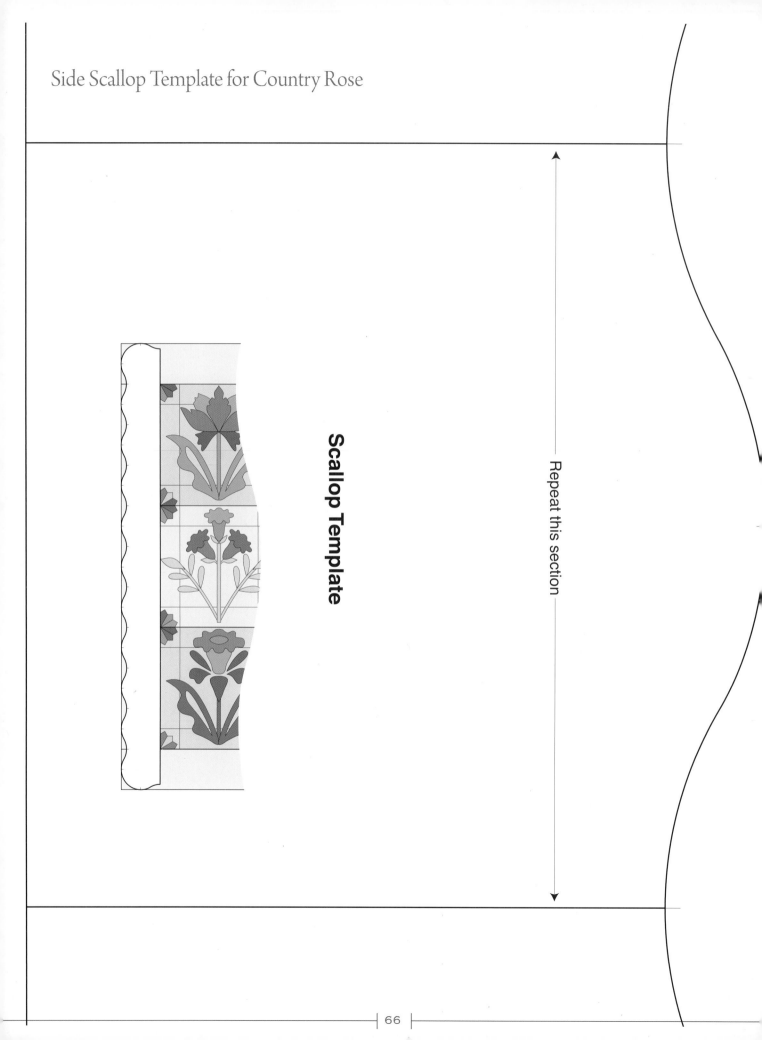

Scallop Template

Repeat this section

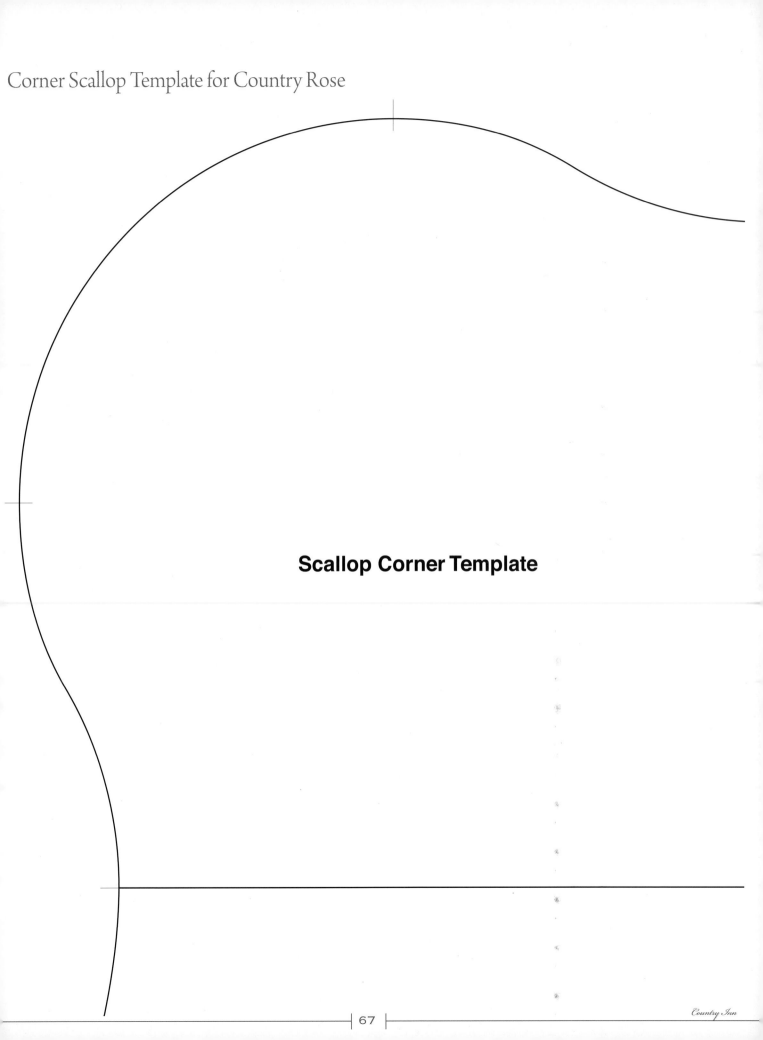

Scallop Corner Template

Finishing for Evening Bloom
Borders

⚜ Cut 76 - 4 1/2" squares for the border.

⚜ Locate the diamond template on page 49. Cut 228 diamonds: 120 from red and 108 from gray fabrics. Refer to the diagram above to determine color placement.

⚜ Sew 3 diamonds together and appliqué them to a 4 1/2" square. Make 76.

⚜ Sew 18 squares together into a strip. Make 2 and sew one to each side of quilt top.

⚜ Sew 20 squares together into a strip. Make 2 and sew one to the top and one to the bottom of the quilt top. Refer to the diagram if necessary.

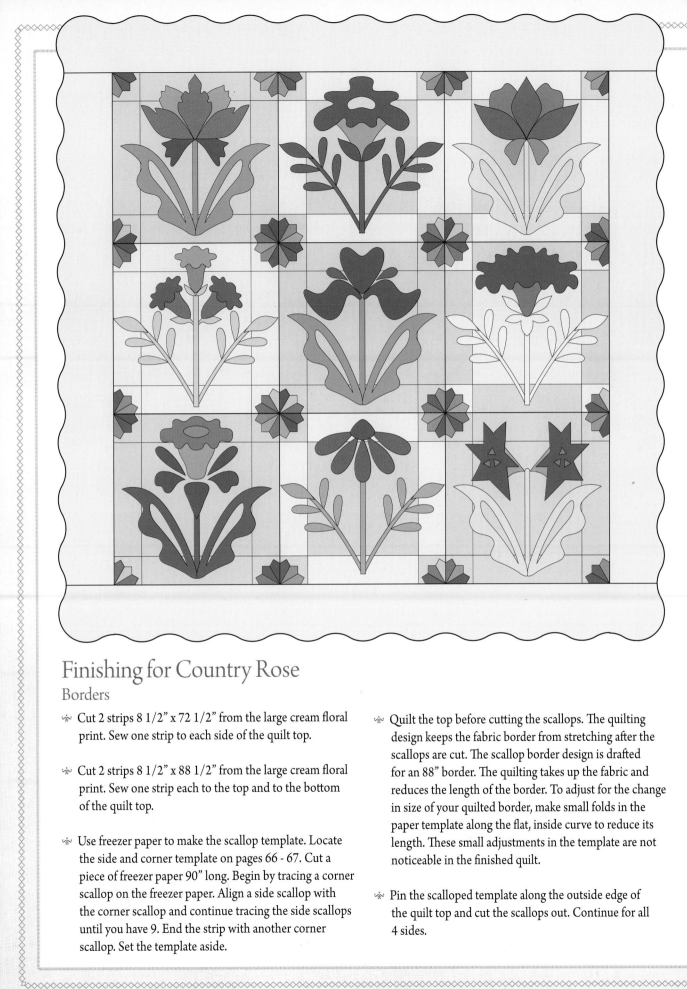

Finishing for Country Rose
Borders

❧ Cut 2 strips 8 1/2" x 72 1/2" from the large cream floral print. Sew one strip to each side of the quilt top.

❧ Cut 2 strips 8 1/2" x 88 1/2" from the large cream floral print. Sew one strip each to the top and to the bottom of the quilt top.

❧ Use freezer paper to make the scallop template. Locate the side and corner template on pages 66 - 67. Cut a piece of freezer paper 90" long. Begin by tracing a corner scallop on the freezer paper. Align a side scallop with the corner scallop and continue tracing the side scallops until you have 9. End the strip with another corner scallop. Set the template aside.

❧ Quilt the top before cutting the scallops. The quilting design keeps the fabric border from stretching after the scallops are cut. The scallop border design is drafted for an 88" border. The quilting takes up the fabric and reduces the length of the border. To adjust for the change in size of your quilted border, make small folds in the paper template along the flat, inside curve to reduce its length. These small adjustments in the template are not noticeable in the finished quilt.

❧ Pin the scalloped template along the outside edge of the quilt top and cut the scallops out. Continue for all 4 sides.

Hexagon Pin Board

Design and sewing by Alma Allen

INSTRUCTIONS

※ Cut a charm square in half twice. The results will be 4 - 2 1/2" squares. Repeat for all of the charm squares. (Or cut 121 - 2 1/2" squares.)

※ Refer to diagram H-1 on page 76 and place the paper hexagon in the center of the wrong side of the fabric square. Fold the edges over and baste into place.

※ Refer to diagram H-2 on page 76 and arrange the hexagons in rows of 11 units each.

※ Refer to diagram H-3 on page 76 and join the edges of the hexagons using a narrow zig zag stitch with the invisible thread on top and cotton thread in the bobbin. Repeat until you have 11 rows of hexagons. Sew the rows together.

※ Layer the piece with batting and backing and quilt.

※ Stretch the piece over a cork board and position in an old frame.

※ Measure the bottom of the frame and evenly measure the space for the 3 drawer pulls. Drill three holes for the knobs and screw them into place

Supply List

※ 1 Charm Pack from Moda Fabrics
※ 121 paper 1" hexagons - Paper Pieces www.paperpieces.com
※ Needle and thread for basting
※ 1 spool of clear MonoPoly thread - size .004 by Superior Threads
※ Batting
※ Backing fabric
※ Old frame - This will determine the number of hexagons needed for this project. The frame I used is 14" x 17"
※ Cork board to fit your frame
※ 3 drawer pulls www.anthropologie.com

...emove stems...
...in a granite stew-pan...
...er until tender (20-40 min...
...chopped, and stew for...
...and pepper, and serve.

...cut them in quarters,
...ender (30-60 min-

...sized parsnips
milk
...and pepper

Young parsnips are most desirable, but old ones...
if the woody center is removed.
Wash and scrape the parsnips, an...
Drain and cut them into...
fat, flour, milk and...
serve.

CREAMED PARSNIPS

...r each onion and parb...
...and remove the centers,
...sion that was scooped ou...
...ft crumbs. Add seasoning...
...ce them in a baking-dish, c...
...nd bake in a hot oven (400°-4...

2 tablespoons flour
2 tablespoons fat

Flea Market Pincushion

Designed and stitched by Alma Allen

INSTRUCTIONS

※ Cut 19 - 2 1/2" squares.

※ Refer to the diagram H-1 on page 76 and place the paper hexagon in the center of the wrong side of the fabric square. Fold the edges over and baste into place.

※ Refer to diagram H-2 on page 76 and arrange the hexagons into rows of 3 units, 4 units, 5 units, 4 units and 3 units each. Join the edges of the hexagons using a narrow zig zag stitch with the invisible thread on top and cotton thread in the bobbin. Refer to diagram H-3 on page 76 and sew the rows together.

※ Layer the piece with batting and backing and quilt.

※ Make a template of the circle from freezer paper. The template is on page 77. Refer to diagram H-4 on page 76 and iron the slick side of the circle on top of the hexagons. Cut out the circle adding a 1/4" seam allowance as you cut.

※ Cut a piece of backing and light weight fusible interfacing the same measurement as the hexagon circle. Iron the interfacing onto the reverse side of the backing.

※ Sew the front to the back, right sides together. Use a 1/4" seam allowance. Leave a 2 1/2" opening for turning.

※ Turn and stuff with crushed walnut shells. Blind stitch the opening closed.

※ Cut a 1 1/2 yd. piece of the pearl cotton. Thread the pearl cotton through a strong needle and knot the end of the thread. Position the needle in the center of the front and push through to the center back. Bring the needle around the pincushion to the top.

※ Pull the thread tightly and again push the needle down through the center front to the back of the pincushion. Bring the needle and thread around to the opposite side of the first thread. The pincushion will now look like it is divided in half. Repeat this process 3 more times. You will have divided the circle into 8 sections. Add the vintage button to the center of the pincushion. Tie the thread off securely.

Supply List

※ Fabric scraps
※ 20 paper 1" hexagons from Paper Pieces www.paperpieces.com
※ Needle and thread for basting
※ 1/4 yd. light weight fusible interfacing
※ 1 spool of clear MonoPoly thread size .004 by Superior Threads
※ 1 large vintage button
※ Pearl Cotton #5 DMC 3328 or DMC 422
※ Scrap of batting
※ Scrap of fabric for backing
※ Crushed walnut shells (bird or lizard litter found at pet stores)

Hexagon template instruction

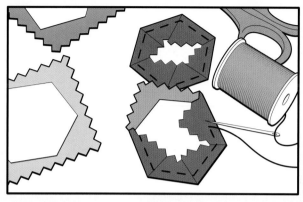

H-1 Fold the edges over and baste into place.

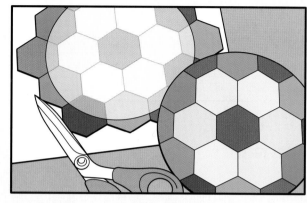

H-4 Use the circle template and trim the hexagons into a circle.

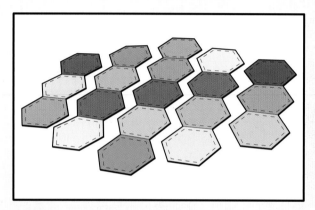

H-2 Arrange the hexagons into rows.

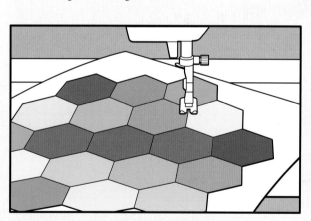

H-3 Join the edges of the hexagons using a narrow zig zag stitch.

TEMPLATE INCLUDES
SEAM ALLOWANCE.

DESIGN SIZE: 114W x 98H

FABRIC: 35ct. Parchment by Weeks Dye Works

SAMPLER SIZE: 6 1/2" x 5 2/3"

SYMBOLS

● CC Little House Brown (DMC 3859/407)

CC - Crescent Colours

Little Red Hen

Designed by Alma Allen
Stitched by B.J. Mardiat and Alma Allen

INSTRUCTIONS

※ Cross stitch with 2 strands of floss over 2 linen threads.

Lavender Sachets

Designed by Alma Allen
Stitched by B.J. Mardiat and Alma Allen
Sewing by Alma Allen

SYMBOLS

♥ WDW Brick (DMC 3857)

◣ CC Jakey Brown (DMC 3859)

✗ CC Chai (DMC 3864)

○ GA Toasted Barley (DMC 642)

CC - Crescent Colours
GA - Gentle Arts
WDW - Weeks Dye Works

"A" Design Size: 20W x 19H
Fabric: 20ct. Cappuccino
by Weeks Dye Works

"J" Design Size: 23W x 29H
Fabric: 35ct. Parchment
by Weeks Dye Works

"L" Design Size: 26W x 22H
Fabric: 35ct. Parchment
by Weeks Dye Works

"M" Design Size: 15W x 21H
Fabric: 28ct. Cashel Autumn Fields

"W" Design Size: 29W x 19H
Fabric: 28ct. gingham natural/straw
by Weeks Dye Works

FINISHED SIZE: 3 3/4" X 3 3/4"

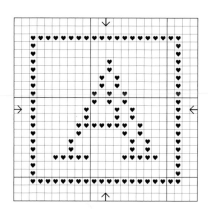

OTHER SUPPLIES

Scraps of fabric for backing
Light weight fusible interfacing
Vintage buttons and trim
Crushed walnut shells
(bird or lizard litter found at pet stores)
Dried lavender flowers

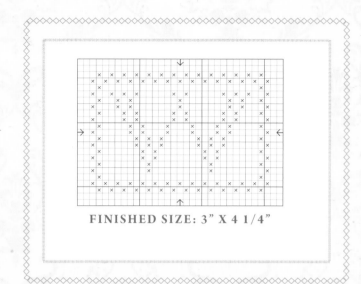

FINISHED SIZE: 3" X 4 1/4"

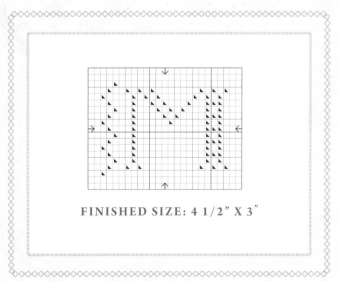

FINISHED SIZE: 4 1/2" X 3"

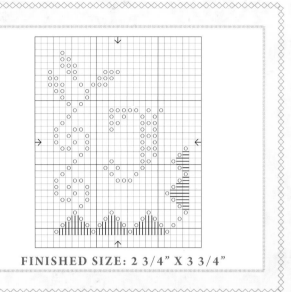

FINISHED SIZE: 2 3/4" X 3 3/4"

SATIN STITCH WITH 2 STRANDS OF TOASTED BARLEY

FINISHED SIZE: 2" X 3 1/2"

Monogrammed Pillowcase

Designed by Barb Adams
Stitched by Barb Adams
Sewing by Leona Adams

SUPPLY LIST

2 1/2 yds. print for the pillowcase
1 yd. for the ruffle and facing
10ct. waste canvas by Charles Craft
1 skein of Lancaster Red (DMC 221) by Weeks Dye Works

Stitch Count: 80W x 17H

INSTRUCTIONS

※ Cut 2 pieces 44" x 36".

※ Fold the fabric for one pillowcase lengthwise, right sides together. Stitch across one end and along the long side. Repeat for the remaining pillowcase.

※ Cut bias strips 3" wide for the ruffle. Sew the strips together until you have 80" in length. Fold the strip in half lengthwise, wrong sides together. Press to crease.

※ Sew the ends of the ruffle together. Gather the bias strip until you have about 44" of ruffle. Baste and pin in place along the outside edge of the pillowcase.

※ Pin the ruffle to the pillowcase and sew using a 1/4" seam allowance.

STANDARD PILLOWCASE

※ Cut bias strips 1 1/2" wide for the facing. Sew the strips together until you have 50" in length.

※ Sew the binding in place. The ruffle will be sandwiched between the pillowcase and the binding. Finish the ends of the binding as if for a quilt. Fold the binding over to the inside of the pillowcase and whip stitch in place.

※ Fold both the pillowcase heading and waste canvas in half to find the centers. Align the centers of both and baste the waste canvas onto the pillowcase. Refer to the picture to assist with placement.

※ Refer to the graph on page 79 and pick the initials you want to stitch on the pillowcase. Lightly pencil them in on the graph provided below.

※ Cross stitch with 2 strands of Lancaster Red floss over 2 canvas threads. When the stitching is complete, remove the canvas threads using the package instructions.

※ Repeat the above instructions for the remaining pillowcase.

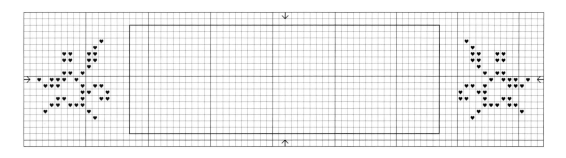

CROSS STITCH DIAGRAM

Vintage Tea Lights

SUPPLY LIST

Vintage shot glasses, cups, or any small glass or tin container that would be appropriate for a candle

Pyrex measuring cup - 2 cup capacity

1 oz. fragrance oil (optional)

2 lb. bag of soy wax

1 package of zinc core wick (ZW-1) - for candles under 2" in diameter

1 package of wick tabs/sustainers

1 small pair of pliers

Hot glue gun and stick of glue

INSTRUCTIONS

※ Clean and dry the container you plan to use.

※ Measure the wick needed. Add an extra 1 1/2" to the wick length for handling. Cut the wick. Thread it through the wick tab/sustainer and crimp to secure the opening with the pliers. Trim the wick on the bottom surface if needed.

※ Put a dot of hot glue on the back of the wick tab and center it in the bottom of the container. The wick needs to be centered so the candle burns evenly.

※ Fill the Pyrex measuring cup with soy wax flakes. Microwave on high for 1 minute. Stir the wax and add more flakes if needed. Microwave on high for another minute. Check the wax to make sure it's melted and ready to use. The wax should be clear.

※ Use a hot pad if needed to remove the container from the microwave.

※ Add fragrance if desired. Stir the melted wax so the oil is absorbed into the wax.

※ Pour the wax slowly into the container. Allow the glass time to absorb the heat.

※ Check the wick placement again to make sure it is centered. Allow time for the wax to cool.

※ Trim the wick.

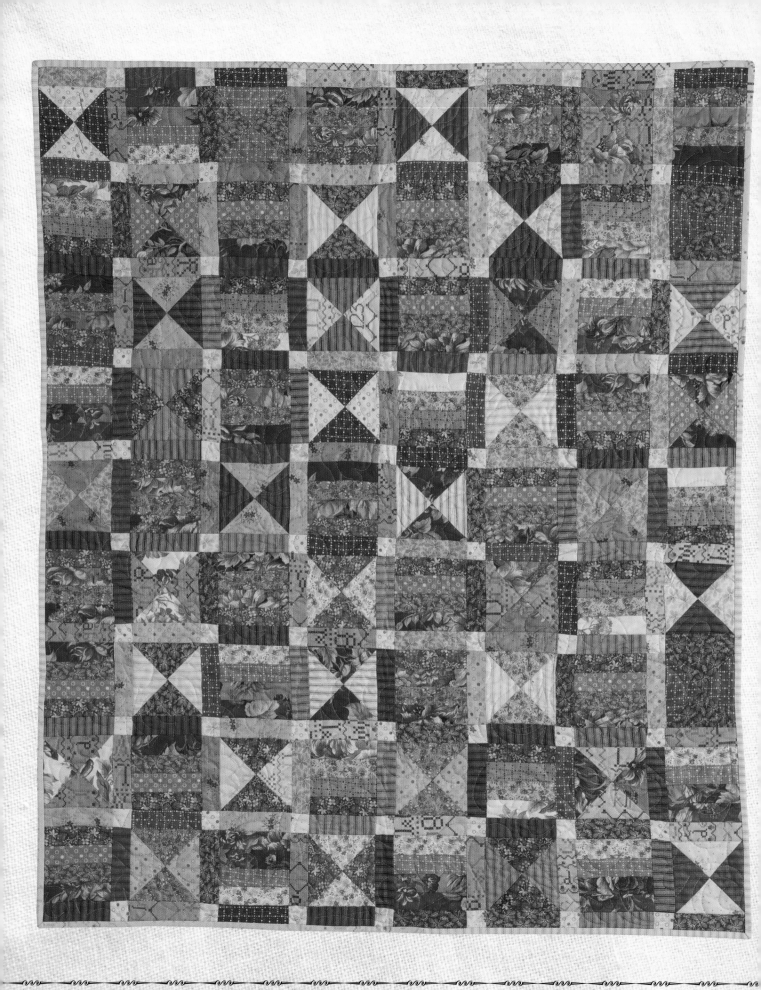

Sweet Thing

Designed and stitched by Jeanne Zyck
Quilting by Jeanne Zyck

PROJECT SIZE 37" X 44"

BLOCK SIZE 3 3/4" FINISHED

SUPPLY LIST

1 Charm pack by Moda fabrics
1 Honeybun by Moda fabrics
3/8 yd. fabric for binding

INSTRUCTIONS

※ Pick up one light and one dark square from the charm pack. Draw a diagonal line down the center of one square. Refer to the diagram below. Placing the 2 squares right sides together, sew a seam 1/4" away from the drawn line. Repeat for the remaining side.

※ Cut the block apart on the drawn line. The results will be 2 half-square triangles. Press each block open.

※ Refer to the diagram above. Note the placement of the blocks. Place 2 half-square triangle blocks right sides together and draw a diagonal line down the center of one block. Again sew 1/4" away from the diagonal line on both sides. Cut the block apart on the drawn line. The results will be 2 hour glass blocks. Your block should measure 4 1/4" square. Make 36 blocks.

※ Sew 4 contrasting Honey Bun strips together using a generous 1/4" seam allowance. Trim into 4 1/4" increments. Your blocks should measure 4 1/4" square. Make 36 blocks.

※ Cut 143 - 4 1/4" strips from the Honey Bun for the sashing. Cut 70 - 1 1/2" squares from the Honey Bun for the corner-stones.

※ Follow the diagram on page 90 and sew the blocks, sashing and cornerstones together.

ASSEMBLY DIAGRAM

Bachelor Buttons

Designed by Barb Adams
Appliqué by Barb Adams and Alma Allen
Sewing by Leona Adams
Quilting by Jeanne Zyck

PROJECT SIZE 72" X 78"

BLOCK SIZE 20" X 22"

Supply List

FOR BACKGROUNDS
2/3 yd. each of 7 different light prints
1 1/2 yds. of a light print for 2 blocks and the binding

FOR APPLIQUÉ PIECES
1/3 yd. each of 9 different pink to red prints
Fat quarter each of 6 different pink to red prints
1/2 yd. each of 6 different green prints

INSTRUCTIONS

FOR EACH BLOCK:

Cutting measurements include a 1/4" seam allowance.

※ Cut 1 - 20 1/2" x 22 1/2" rectangle from a background print.

※ Locate the placement diagram on page 94. Note the templates needed for this block. Refer to the photo for color placement.

※ Cut out the shapes, adding a 1/8" - 1/4" seam allowance. Refer to the diagram and baste the pieces in place on the background block.

※ Appliqué the pieces to the background.

※ Repeat for 9 blocks.

FOR THE BORDER:

※ Cut 46 - 6 1/2" squares from the background prints.

※ Locate the placement diagram on page 96. Note the template needed for this block. Refer to the photo for color placement.

※ Cut out the shapes, adding a 1/8" - 1/4" seam allowance. Refer to the diagram and baste the pieces in place on the background block.

※ Appliqué the pieces to the background.

※ Make 46 blocks.

※ Sew 2 strips each of 11 blocks. Sew one strip to each side of the quilt top.

※ Sew 2 strips each of 12 blocks. Sew one strip to the top and one to the bottom of the quilt top.

One square = 1"

K
Cut 10

J
Cut 13

I
Cut 5

D
Cut 1

G
Cut 1

Bachelor Buttons

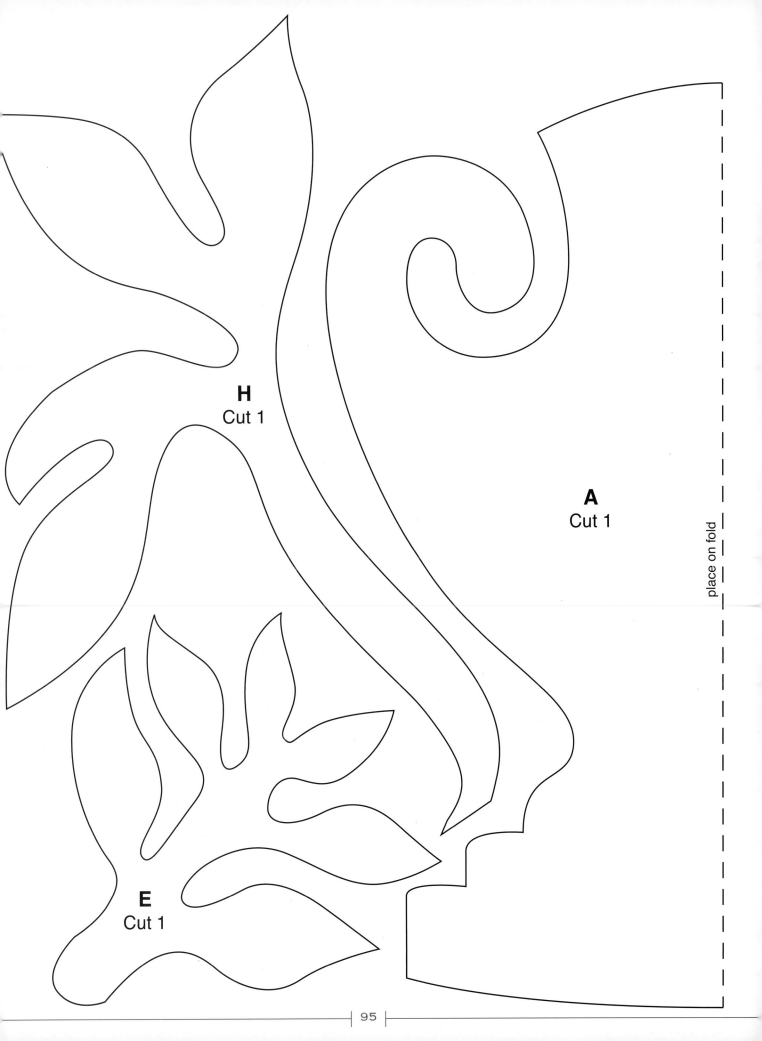

H
Cut 1

A
Cut 1

place on fold

E
Cut 1

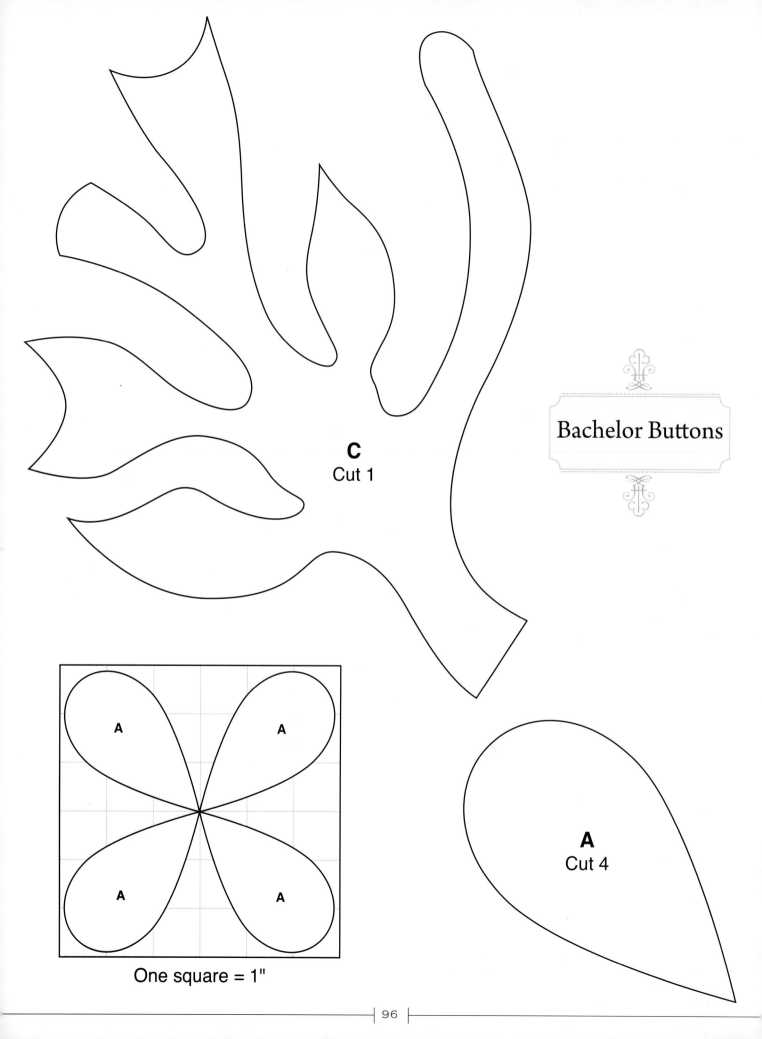

C
Cut 1

Bachelor Buttons

A
A
A
A

One square = 1"

A
Cut 4

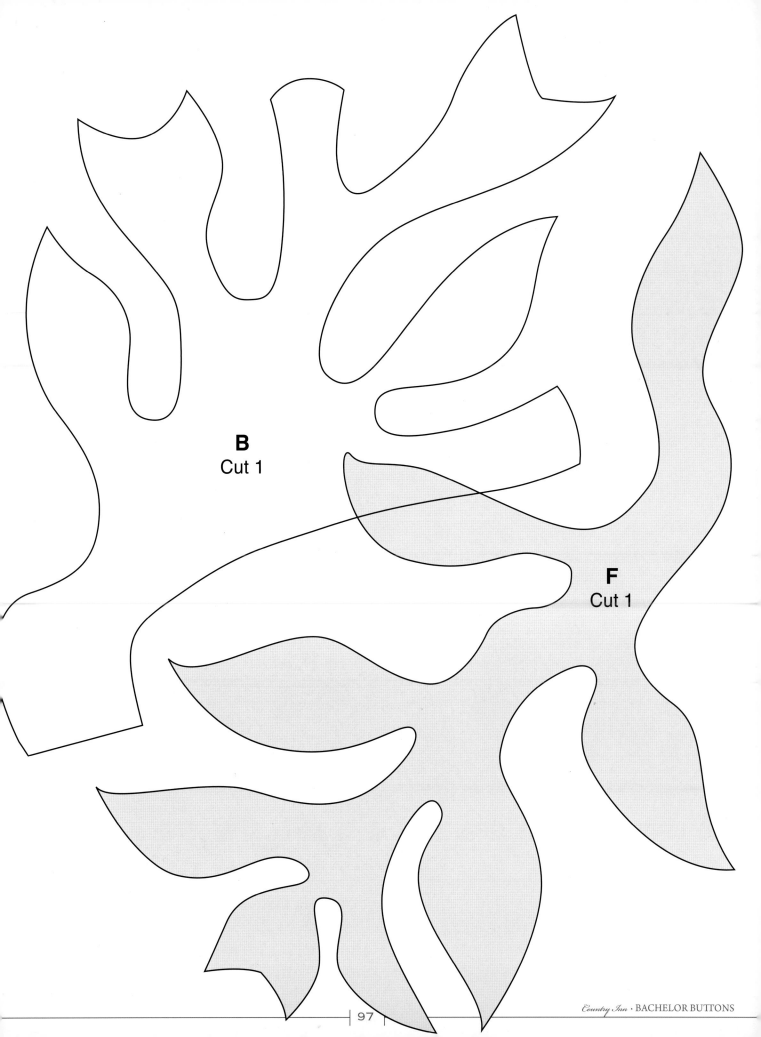

B
Cut 1

F
Cut 1

BACHELOR BUTTONS SEWING DIAGRAM

Shooting Stars

Design by Barb Adams
Appliqué by Leona Adams
Quilted by Jeanne Zyck

PROJECT SIZE 85" X 85"
BLOCK SIZE 6" FINISHED

INSTRUCTIONS

Cutting measurements include a 1/4" seam allowance.

※ Cut 169 - 6 1/2" squares from an assortment of the background prints.

※ Locate the star pattern on page 103. Refer to the photo and diagram on page 102 for color placement.

※ Make a template of the star shape. Cut out the shape, adding 1/8" - 1/4" seam allowance. Refer to the diagram and baste the star in place on the background block.

※ Appliqué the star to the background. Make 169 star blocks.

 Set these aside.

Supply List

1 yd. each of 6 different light tan and blue prints for the backgrounds
2/3 yd. each of 4 different red prints for stars and stripes
1/2 yd. each of 4 different blue prints for stars and stripes
1 yd. of a blue small check for the setting triangles
2/3 yd. of a blue print for the binding

THE PIECED BLOCKS

※ Cut 2 - 2 1/2" x 6 1/2" strips from red prints.

※ Cut 1 - 2 1/2" x 6 1/2" strip of a light print. Refer to the pieced block diagram on page 103. Sew the block together. Make 12.

THE SETTING TRIANGLES

※ Cut 9 - 9 3/4" squares from the blue small check fabric. Cut each square in half twice on the diagonal to make 36 side triangles.

※ Cut 2 - 5 1/8" squares. Cut each in half once on the diagonal to make 4 corner triangles.

※ Refer to the sewing diagram and sew the blocks together.

SHOOTING STARS PLACEMENT DIAGRAM

PIECED BLOCK DIAGRAM

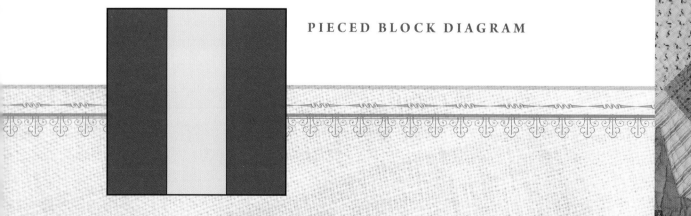

Star
Cut 169

Pot of Posies

Design by Barb Adams
Appliqué by Leona Adams

Supply List

WOOL FOR BACKGROUND AND APPLIQUÉ

1/2 yd. of a light taupe tweed for background

12" x 6" piece of a light cream and tan small check for the basket

14" x 6" piece of a red paisley for the flowers and leaves

10" x 6" piece of a red plaid for the flowers and leaves

14" x 6" each of 2 different dark yellow green pieces for the stems and leaves

6" x 6" piece of a light gold for leaves

6" x 4" piece of a different gold for leaves

6" x 6" piece of a blue grey for the leaves

28" x 10" piece of a red plaid for the border detail

OTHER SUPPLIES

1/2 yd. light taupe print for backing

Tacky glue

Floss to match the appliqué

Freezer paper for templates

PROJECT SIZE 42" X 18"

INSTRUCTIONS

※ Trace each portion of the background template on one large piece of freezer paper. One half of the background template is on pages 106 - 109.

※ Make templates of the appliqué shapes. Refer to the templates and cut out the pieces needed.

※ Cut the stems in 1/4" wide strips. Refer to the placement diagram and position them on the light taupe tweed.

※ Use tacky glue to baste the pieces in place.

※ Appliqué the pieces with a whip stitch. Use one strand of floss or regular sewing thread.

※ Tear the red wool plaid into 5 - 2" x 28" strips. Trace the scalloped edge template onto freezer paper. Cut out the template and iron it to the beginning of the strip. Cut around the template shape. Peel away the template and iron it again along the strip. Continue to cut out the template until the 28" strip is scalloped. Repeat for the remaining strips. Place the scalloped strips onto the backside of the mat. Whip stitch them in place.

※ Cut the light taupe print for the backing. Add 1/4" to the background template as you cut out the fabric. Center the penny mat onto the backing and baste in place. Turn under a 1/4" seam allowance and blind stitch the fabric backing to the wool piece.

PLACEMENT DIAGRAM

▼Join here-B▼

▼Join here-A▼

Pot of Posies

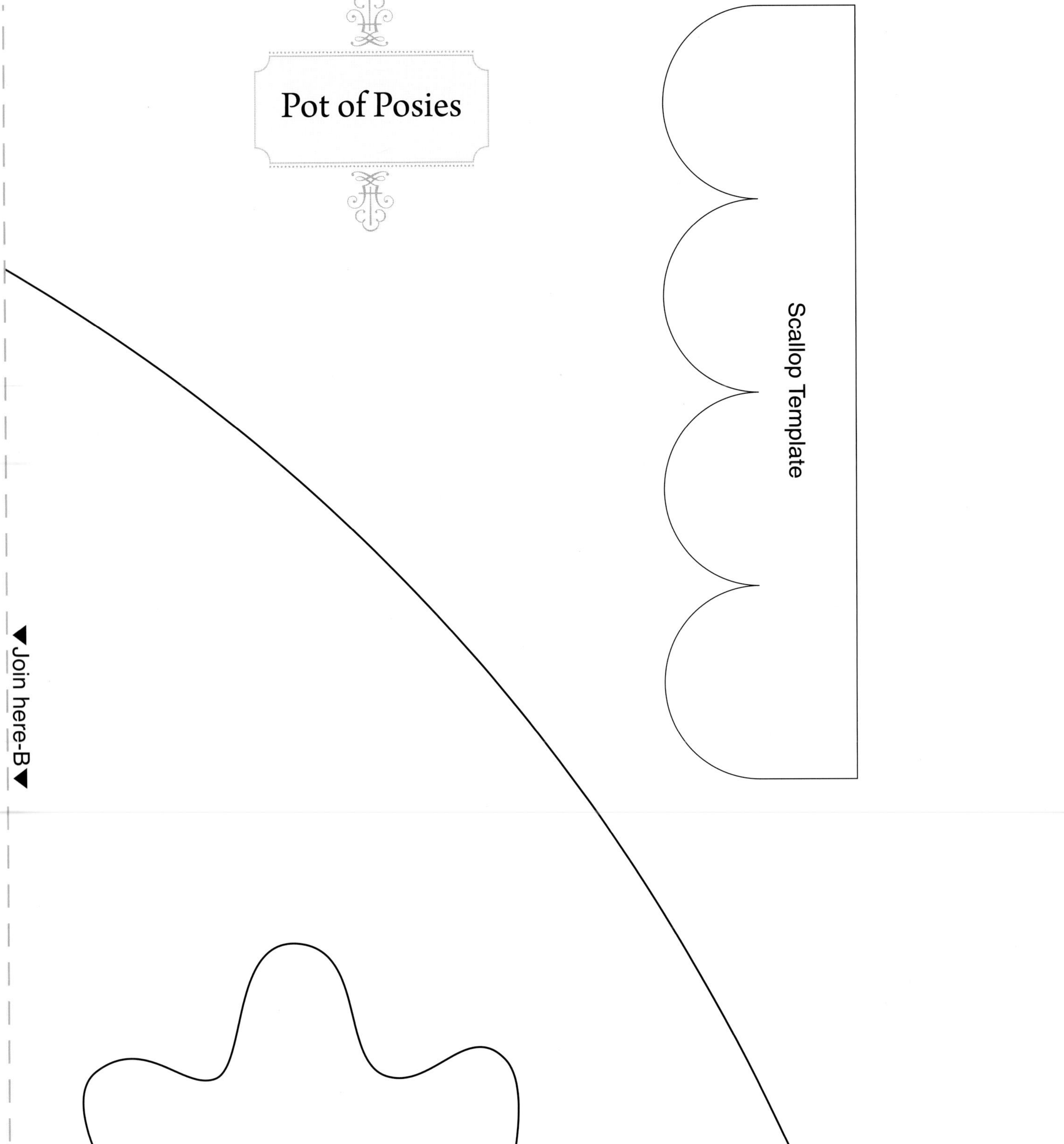

Scallop Template

Join here-C▼

▲Join here-C▲

▲ Join here-A ▲

▶ Join here-D ▶

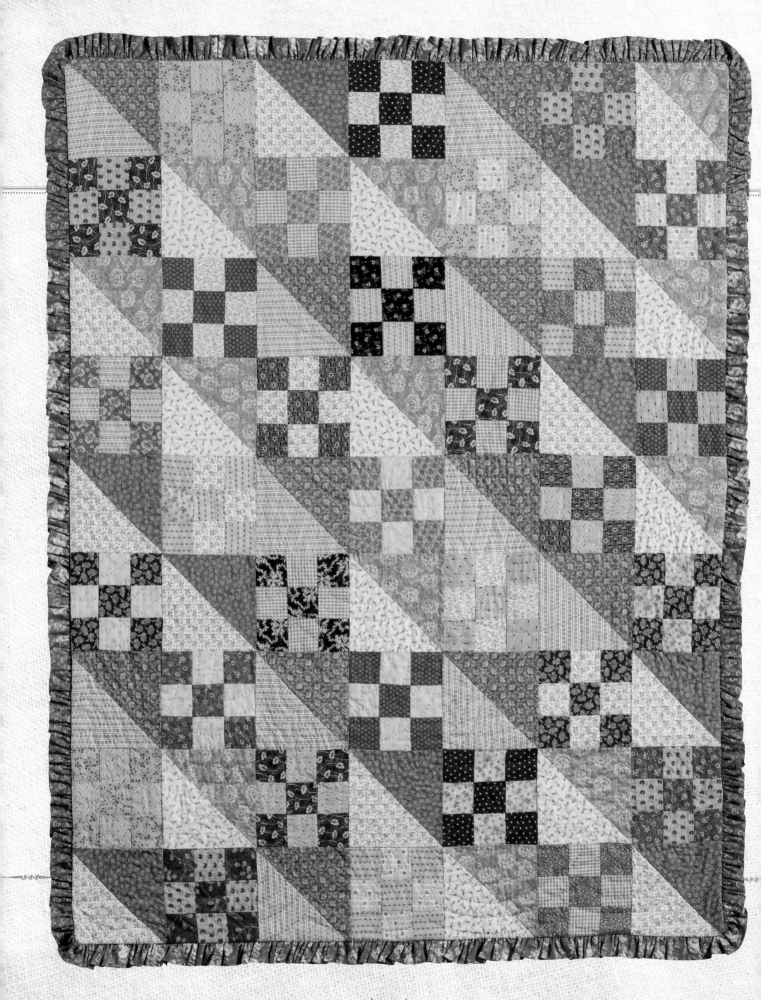

Country Charm

Designed and stitched by Alma Allen
Quilted by Alma Allen

Supply List

1/3 yd. each of 4 different light prints for the 9-patch and the half-square triangle blocks

2 1/2" strips of 8 different light prints for the 9-patch blocks

2 1/2" strips of 14 different dark prints for the 9-patch blocks

1/2 yd. of 1 teal print, 1/4 yd. each of 2 other teal prints for the half-square triangle units

7/8 yd. of a brown and teal floral print for the ruffle

2 yds. of a light print for the binding and backing

PROJECT SIZE 42" X 54"

BLOCK SIZE 6" FINISHED

INSTRUCTIONS

Cutting measurements include a 1/4" seam allowance.

※ Cut 124 - 2 1/2" squares from an assortment of the light strips.

※ Cut 155 - 2 1/2" squares from an assortment of the dark strips.

※ Piece 31 - 9-patch blocks.

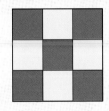

※ Cut 16 - 6 7/8" squares from the 3 teal prints.

※ Cut 16 - 6 7/8" squares from the 4 different light prints.

※ Refer to the diagram at right. Draw a diagonal line down the center of one teal square. Pick up a light square and place the 2 squares together with right sides facing. Sew a seam 1/4" away from the drawn line. Repeat for the remaining side.

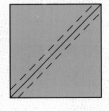

※ Cut the block apart on the drawn line. The results will be 2 half-square triangles. Press each block open. Make 32 half-square triangles.

※ Refer to the picture and sew the top together.

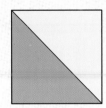

THE RUFFLED EDGING

※ Quilt the quilt before adding the ruffle.

※ Cut 8 - 3 1/2" x 45" strips. Sew the strips together. Press in half lenghwise. Gather the ruffle. Baste in place along the edge of the quilt top.

※ Cut 6 - 1 3/4" x 45" strips. Sew the strips together. This strip will be the binding. Sew the strip on, sandwiching the ruffle between the quilt top and the binding. Turn the binding towards the back, turn under your seam allowance and whip stitch in place.